distributed

JAVA™ 2

platform Database Development

SUN MICROSYSTEMS PRESS
A PRENTICE HALL TITLE

STEWART BIRNAM

Prentice Hall books are widely used by corporations and government agencies for training, marketing, and resale.

The publisher offers discounts on this book when ordered in bulk quantities. For more information, contact Corporate Sales Department, Phone: 800-382-3419; FAX: 201- 236-7141; E-mail: corpsales@prenhall.com

Or write: Prentice Hall PTR, Corporate Sales Dept., One Lake Street, Upper Saddle River, NJ 07458.

Editorial/production supervision: Jane Bonnell
Cover design director: Jerry Votta
Cover design: Talar Agasyan
Cover illustration: Karen Strelecki
Composition: Ronnie Bucci
Manufacturing manager: Alexis R. Heydt
Acquisitions editor: Gregory G. Doench
Editorial assistant: Mary Treacy
Marketing manager: Debby vanDijk

Sun Microsystems Press:
Marketing manager: Michael Llwyd Alread
Publisher: Rachel Borden

10   9   8   7   6   5   4   3   2   1

ISBN 0-13-026861-5

Sun Microsystems Press
A Prentice Hall Title

To my family—Alida, Ian, Rachel, and Grace—and to my in-laws—Lily and Ray Mow—for their love and support even when I'm not writing techno-babble.

To my techno-posse: Mike Thompson and his DBA kung fu; Andy Hendrickson and the inspiration of his 30fps volumetric renderer, which made me want to learn Java in the first place; George Cook for introducing me to "Cascading Cheeses"; Rich Burdon and his "Brain"; Lori Casler for saying, "Why don't you write a book, then I wouldn't have to write all this stuff down. Is that your phone ringing? Weren't you just paged? Oh, look at the time!"; and Lisa Hoffman for saying, "Don't make it funny. I hate that."

Contents

Chapter 1

• •

Chapter 2
• •

··

Chapter 3
··

The RMI Server, 51

Chapter 4

Chapter 5

Programming Concepts, 99

The UnitDbServlet, 101

Chapter 6

The Command-Line Client—Providing Simplified Access to Your Database API, 115

Quick Start, 115

Technology Overview, 115

Programming Techniques, 116

Conclusion, 121

Chapter 9

Monitoring Tools and System Calls, 155

Appendix A

Javadoc API Documentation for the Classes Used in This Book, 165

List of Code Examples

Preface

Quick Start

This book covers JDBC, RMI, Swing, servlets, and command-line programs and how to tie them all together to build a system using an Oracle database and the Linux operating system. The first few chapters are mostly background information on multitiered systems. Subsequent chapters cover specific technologies and how you can reuse code used to access a database in Swing applications or servlets.

Oracle is used exclusively in all the examples that have to do with accessing a database. Examples of simple querying as well as complex joins are covered. Inserts, updates, and deletes of regular data—as well as how to store Web images as BLOBS in the database—are all shown in detail. Oracle-specific features of SQL, such as use of the CONNECT BY statement in hierarchical tables, is shown. Displaying parent-child relationships in GUIs via the Swing Jtree object is explained.

All the example code was developed on Red Hat Linux 6.1, although the code would work on any Java 1.1 capable platform, which is just about everything these days. Particular attention is given to crafting shell scripts and makefiles to make deployment and development easier. The Oracle database is version 8, running under Linux. Examples of making system calls to Unix commands, as well as building sysadmin remote monitoring tools, are also given.

Introduction

Many books on Java technology exist in the marketplace. A good chunk of these are aimed at teaching the fundamentals of the language. The rest take the tack of choosing a particular API and providing an in-depth tour. Very few of these books tell you how to integrate all these APIs and technologies and actually build a deployable system. Even fewer books talk about solving very specific problems, like accessing an Oracle database. In fact, I couldn't find a single example of this, and I looked very, very hard.

Faced with having to get the job done, I ended up as many before me have: embarking on a massive research project to find and accumulate all the information and techniques I needed to build the application I wanted to build. Having done that, I decided that others might be saved the trouble I went through, by sharing the knowledge that I found hiding in so many nooks and crannies. So I wrote this book.

This book is about building systems with Java technology. Building successful real-world systems involves more than just an efficient algorithm or some clever coding tricks. It means building scalable, efficient, maintainable code, that may or may not integrate an existing system or software package, such as Oracle. With the prevalence of the Internet, your software will most certainly need to make use of the Internet and utilize established Internet protocols. In addition, you need to be able to efficiently administer, deploy, and document your system in a timely manner. Without good administration or deployment, your system is unusable and probably perceived as unstable as well.

My intent is to show you how you can solve these problems, as well as address the actual application issues, with a combination of open standards and Java technology. To illustrate these concepts, technologies, and their use, we will build a *distributed database application system* that uses an Oracle database.

With all the industry buzz concerning Linux recently, I set out to see if all these techniques could be applied under Linux. I'm glad to report that the Java implementations under Linux are strong and robust. Oracle now has a release of their database for Linux as well. In the last few months, all of the "gotchas" that came with deploying Java under Linux have been resolved. Java runs under Linux without any significant differences from any other Unix platform.

Why a Distributed Database Application System?

Distributed computing is becoming more prevalent, thanks to the Internet and the proliferation of cheap PCs. It's no secret that the Internet is changing our lives. One interesting side effect of everyone's great interest in the Internet is the amount of computing power that now sits mostly idle, waiting for someone to click on a Web page or strike a key. Furthermore, never before has it been possible to acquire so much computer for so little price. With the network gluing all these machines together, it's now possible and important to consider distributing problems across multiple heterogeneous computers.

Database application development is by nature distributed, and almost all companies and organizations have a need for database access. A database is something you want to share. The number of people and organizations you may want to share it with may vary, but chances are the information needs to move across and be accessed by multiple systems. Even if you're implementing a two-tiered database model today, you're still distributing the work by moving the presentation layer off the server and to the client. It's an attractive idea to make the client do more work, thus enabling your server to service a greater number of requests by offloading more of its workload to the client.

Delivering a working distributed database application system calls for the integration of many APIs and technologies. You can understand all the reasons for wanting a distributed application, but implementing one requires a knowledge of networking, database programming, systems administration, GUI programming, systems programming, and Web programming—all areas in which there isn't typically a lot of skills overlap. Individuals specializing in one discipline may have almost no knowledge or experience with another. It can be difficult to pull together a team that can cover all the bases. It can be even harder to coordinate all their efforts efficiently toward the completion of a common goal.

Java has a huge collection of APIs that address all these areas and more. While other languages offer similar capabilities, I can think of no other that provides so many useful and well-documented classes as part of their core API.

Companies and organizations have an increasing need to access data from potentially distant and heterogeneous systems. E-commerce dictates the need for organizations to communicate with each other without the necessity of identical hardware or software. Java technology, with its strength in network programming and cross-platform "write once run anywhere" capabilities, is uniquely suited to address this problem. In addition, scientific and technical computing can also benefit from this technology by enabling collaboration all over the world.

Today's market requires flexible systems to respond to swiftly changing needs of the organization and consumers. The pace of technology and systems today is astonishing. It is fairly evident that in order to maintain any kind of production environment you will always be integrating new technology with old, and new systems with existing systems. In addition, not only may your systems be changing rapidly due to technical reasons, but you may also be changing the way that you do business just as rapidly. Your systems need to be designed in such a way to accommodate this. Object-oriented programming and Java technologies can help you build systems toward this goal.

You may still have to leverage the existing systems and resources. Many companies and organizations today still require expensive legacy systems, or have legacy applications in place for some departments because of a vertical application and/or significant training investment. Often there are also political factors as to why one technology is adopted over another, and those technologies may change from department to department. Spreadsheets, e-mail, text files, and databases all abound as individuals in the organization build their own systems based on their needs and skill levels.

Typically in this environment, you may have programmers scattered across the organization, coding in a variety of languages on multiple platforms. In an early effort to get information to flow from one division to another, several patchwork systems may have evolved. This kept things moving, but as the needs of the organization changed, it became harder and harder to implement new systems for fear of breaking the old ones. Not to mention that not everyone may be comfortable with dropping his or her system in favor of someone else's, and potentially losing the control they may have had.

A key focus of this book is the belief that systems need to be able to react swiftly to the changing needs of the organization. Their architecture needs to be designed to reflect this. Many organizations—including startups, nonprofits, media, scientific/ engineering environments, and others—may also have the additional constraint of limited budget and/or nontraditional business models that make out-of-the-box solutions impossible or prohibitively expensive. Moreover, it may be necessary to integrate many types of data storage methods in an effort to bring the departments together into a centralized information base.

Can Java Technology Help Me Build Systems?

This book is an answer to that question, and sets out to design a new system that maintains flexibility while respecting the needs of various users. We accomplish this by building and designing our business applications and systems with Java technology using a distributed computing model. Java's strength as a network programming language, its cross-platform nature, and ability to interface natively with many vendor databases make the entire thing possible. Furthermore, the almost daily addition of more APIs for the Java environment makes its use more attractive than ever. Literally every facet of computing is covered, from XML to 3D, sound to Jini. There has never been a more widely used and supported set of APIs. Not to mention that most of these APIs have accessible source.

Intended Audience

Are you:

- thinking of designing a distributed database system?

- in charge of an IS/IT department?

- a software developer looking to get an insight into some new technologies in order to help solve a particular problem?

- a budding programmer who's tired of poring over simple examples, and wants to see how everything integrates into a single, breathing system?

If any one of these is you, then this book will help.

If you're a software developer, this book will serve as a guide in building distributed systems. If you're a systems administrator, it will help you understand what the administration and maintenance issues for systems like these are. If you're an IT/IS manager, you can get a good understanding of the requirements in these kinds of systems, that will help you develop strategies and staffing/budget requirements for your projects.

Whichever focus you have, this book will help you understand how all these complex issues blend together to build a system. Even if you decide not to do the core development yourself, but rather integrate turnkey solutions instead, you will be in a better position to evaluate those systems and perhaps even write the "glue" to hold them together after reading this book.

Organization of This Book

In the beginning of each chapter you will find a quick outline in case you want to skip through, or quickly find some code snippet or piece of wisdom. Several chapters will have sections devoted to technology overviews, programming, administration, and support and deployment where relevant. In this way you will be able to safely skim through sections that may not be critical to you.

For programmers, rather than take you on a tour of the various API specifications, I'm going to assume you're already familiar with the core API. That is, you've looked at other books in this series, have tried out some of the examples, but are still wondering how it all fits together. To that end you'll see throughout this book how the various Java APIs are brought together to create something real. In this respect alone, you may find this book valuable even if you don't intend to implement a complete system yourself. Understanding the fundamentals of how all the various components fit together will aid you tremendously in your evaluation of third-party solutions and/or development libraries.

In addition, I'll show you how to integrate the software you build with existing, well-known open source and commercial systems. By the end of this book, you should have all the information you need to decide what pieces of the system you'll have to build and what pieces you can integrate. To get the most out of this book, you should have some familiarity with:

- Relational databases

- SQL (Structured Query Language—a nonprocedural language used to extract information out of databases)

- JDBC (Java Database Connectivity—part of the 1.1 and greater core API)

- HTTP

- NFS (Network File System—commonly used file sharing scheme under Unix)

- FTP

- Samba (An SMB system that runs on Unix servers, making it possible to share files to Win32 machines)

- SMTP (Simple Mail Transport Protocol—the underlying protocol for Internet e-mail)

The Road Ahead

In Chapter 1, we'll describe a distributed database solution implemented entirely in Java. It gives a high-level view of the server configuration, how the broker works, and how the various clients interact with the system. It focuses on hardware independence, and provides guidelines for determining the price/performance ratio of your system.

Chapter 2 details the building of a database API to abstract the nuts and bolts of the database for the application programmer. We'll deal with ways you can encapsulate your SQL into an API.

Chapter 3 deals with the construction of an RMI server, along with tips on how to administer it.

Chapter 4 starts the discussion of client development by building a Swing application using the database API. General issues of using remote objects and Swing are discussed, with special attention to exception handling. Examples are given specific to populating GUI components with data from the database, like Lists, Tables, Trees, and ComboBoxes.

Chapter 5 gives us a taste of how nice it is to be able to reuse your software by delivering access to the same database API via servlets. We also give a brief tour of the Apache JServ and Java Web Server from an administration and development perspective.

Chapter 6 lets us now gorge ourselves in reusability by building a command-line client to provide an even easier way for script programmers or Web developers to access your database API.

Chapter 7 shows you how to make your software distribution simple, and save you from walking to each machine and installing it. This is accomplished by some very well-known services (HTTP, FTP, NFS, and Samba), and some clever systems architecture and scripts.

Chapter 8 gives a how-to on reading and writing BLOBS (Binary Large Objects) to the database. Special attention is given to delivering images and other multimedia content from BLOBs to servlets and applications.

Chapter 9 illustrates how to build your own monitoring tools to help your administrators and support staff, as well as how to make system calls accessible via RMI.

Running the Example Code

All the examples in this book were developed and tested under Red Hat Linux 6.1. The database used was Oracle 8 for Linux. The JVM was the 1.1.8 Implementation for Linux from IBM. The examples were also tested with the Blackdown.org 1.1.6v5 JDK and with the Sun/Blackdown 1.2.2 Release Candidate 2.

Check the following Web sites to download your own JDK for Linux:

- *www.ibm.com/java*—JDK 1.1.8 and JDK 1.3

- *www.blackdown.org*—JDK 1.1.6v5 (the implementation preferred by Oracle)

- *java.sun.com*—JDK 1.2.2

Of course the examples will run under Windows NT, Windows 98, and Solaris as well. Oracle software is naturally available for NT, Solaris, and other flavors of Unix. You can download the Linux or other versions on a trial basis at *technet.oracle.com*.

Oracle also makes a version of their software for Windows 95 and 98 called Oracle Lite, which you can use if you want to try the examples on that platform. Oracle Lite has a different JDBC driver than the regular Oracle database. Make sure you consult the documentation.

If you're using a 1.1 JVM, you'll need to download the Swing libraries separately. You can find these at *java.sun.com/jfc*.

The servlet examples were developed against Apache JServ 1.1b2 and run with the Apache Web Server 1.3.9, again under Linux. Apache JServ is an implementation of the 2.0 Java servlet specification. Sun is working with the Apache community and supporting the Jakarta effort that implements the 2.2 spec. Find out more about it at *jakarta.apache.org* or at Sun's Web site *java.sun.com*. There is a README file in the source distribution that will guide you in getting the examples running.

## Chapter 1

Distributed Database Application Design

▼ QUICK START
▼ TECHNOLOGY OVERVIEW
▼ DATABASE APPLICATION MODELS
▼ TWO-TIER MODEL
▼ N-TIER MODEL
▼ COMPARING BOTH MODELS
▼ MIGRATING TO A MULTITIER ARCHITECTURE

Quick Start

This chapter covers background information about multitier systems and their architecture. Its intent is to provide a foundation for programmers and managers toward understanding distributed systems. If you already have a good handle on these issues, you can safely skip ahead to Chapter 2.

Technology Overview

Understanding the System

Building a distributed database application is more than just simple application development. It means understanding how systems interact with each other over networks. It means finding out under what conditions the database performs optimally. It means understanding the strengths and weaknesses of all the components in your system and trying to distribute the problem across those systems in a way that yields the greatest performance.

1

Therefore, unless you're starting from scratch it's going to take a fair amount of analysis to find out which parts of your existing system are worth keeping and where the bottlenecks are. Furthermore, costs and existing systems requirements may affect how you build your system. In all cases it's going to be a case of tipping the scales in one direction or another in order to achieve the best performance with the most flexibility.

Java technology is uniquely suited to address this complex problem. Whether you're tying together existing systems or building completely new ones, using Java technology will enable you to build stable, complex systems in a relatively short development cycle. However, before you start coding you'll want an understanding of the hardware issues in a distributed system. The purpose of this chapter is to acquaint you with some hardware scenarios that may affect how you develop your application, and to review traditional models of database computing so that you can weight the advantages of a distributed system for yourself, and to make sure you're familiar with some of the terminology.

Hardware and Network Configurations

Prior to building your system, you'll need a clear understanding of what servers and workstations you have in your current environment and how they are networked together (100BaseT vs. 10BaseT vs. gigabit Ethernet? LAN/WAN? Firewalls? Proxies?). Also important is what operating system runs on these various machines. It's not uncommon that your servers and workstations run different operating systems. It's also getting more mainstream to have alternative operating systems (non-Win32) on client systems based on application demands. Particularly with the rising popularity of alternative operating systems you may find workstations not solely Win32 but a combination of Solaris, Linux, FreeBSD, Win32 and MacOS. Servers may run Solaris, Tru64, AIX, IRIX, etc., or even Linux and FreeBSD. It's my belief that this diversification will continue as greater application demands force homogenous computing environments to become more heterogeneous. Whether they do or not you'll be prepared to take advantage of them by using Java technology. As of this writing, I have been able to find and use at least a 1.1 implementation of Java on FreeBSD, Linux (Intel and Alpha), HPUX, AIX, Irix, Tru64, MacOS, and of course, Solaris and Win32.

Finding the Bottlenecks

Once you've outlined what you have, it may become clear that there are several bottlenecks in the current operating environment that you can't overcome easily, or have the budget to change right away. Knowing these will help you decide if you'll need to try to address the problems with your software.

Planning for Tomorrow

You'll also need to plan for the future by designing your system to be flexible enough to handle change. Will the Linux server in use today be replaced by a Solaris server next year? Will a percentage of your Win32 systems be replaced with Linux? If any pieces of your system are platform dependent, then you may be setting yourself up for a problem later. For example, if you use a third-party application server or other piece of middleware, then you may always be limited to the operating systems that the vendor supports. Or if you decide to use Java 2, then you will be limited to the platforms and other software that support it currently.

For example, the Oracle 8i database has a built-in Java Virtual Machine for use in server-side applications. This JVM is optimized for the database and can be used to get more performance out of online transaction processing applications. The JVM is based on Java 1.1.6, so if you're planning on taking advantage of this technology, you'll want to consider the potential problems of maintaining two different versions of Java in your application framework.

As of this writing, only the 1.1 version of Java is available for all platforms. There are many alpha and beta versions of Java 2 available on other platforms besides Win32 and Solaris, so the development effort is under way. But if you want to write reliable, deployable software today, you'll have to use Java 1.1. Fortunately, that doesn't exclude you from much on the server side, and many features of Java 2 like Swing or JNDI have separate packages available that can be used from Java 1.1.

Bridging Systems

Two things are going to connect your systems together: the network, and Java technology. Make sure ahead of time that you have access to all the machines you want to bridge together. For instance, you may need to access proxies to communicate with other systems. You may have free access to some systems, but the systems are so busy you may need to transact with them in as low-impact a way as possible. Finding out in advance will help you design your system that much better.

Database Application Models

Let's do a quick overview of popular Database Application Models so that we can get a clear understanding of some of the systems issues that lie ahead. One weakness of many database developers is to leave the hardware and systems planning to the systems administrators. This leaves a huge gap between hardware and software issues that neither parties have the resources to resolve. It's your responsibility as a developer to build a reasonable system for someone to administer. Doing that requires a basic understanding of how these kinds of systems are typically architected.

Toward that end, we provide an overview of typical database application models. We cover basic hardware and networking issues in an effort to build awareness on the part of the developer and as a guide for your system design.

Two-tier Model

Many database applications use a two-tier model. In fact, many systems you find in production today are implemented using this model, as it is relatively simple to implement and design. The basic structure is illustrated in Figure 1–1.

Hardware Configurations

Most systems of this model have a midrange to large database server. Typically, this is a multiprocessor machine running some flavor of Unix supported by the database vendor. Usually, a lot of time and money has been poured into this system. (Multiple CPU machines are generally fairly expensive.) The organization has decided that it's imperative that it be up and running 24/7. This is the first place performance enhancements are attempted, so it is most likely as well-tuned as it can be—or at least you hope so. Just as likely, because of its cost, it may be as good as it's going to get, so it's your job to start making it work more efficiently without spending lots of money.

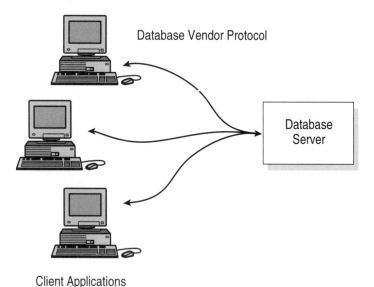

Figure 1–1: The two-tiered database model

TIP: If you do have some money left to spend, the best improvement you can make is to purchase additional memory. This can dramatically increase performance in database applications, provided you have a skilled DBA who can tune the database to take advantage of the additional memory.

Network Topology

In this model, the client software maintains a direct persistent connection to the database throughout the life of the application. This connection remains alive whether or not the user is actively using the application. The connection is often composed of a vendor protocol (like SQLNet for Oracle) riding on top of a transport protocol (like TCP/IP or DECNet). This makes it a rather heavyweight connection between client and server. The vendor protocol might be doing continuous error checking and connection monitoring in addition to whatever the transport protocol is already providing. To most database application developers, this is a logical and totally expected state of affairs, and nothing to be concerned about. However, as you can see, there is a fair amount of overhead going into just maintaining the connection. These days, when a typical user may have several network-aware applications running at once (Netscape, e-mail, etc.), this drain on resources is something that is going to effect workstation performance. On some operating systems, it might even cause the workstation to crash.

Administration

In order to deploy an application using this model, each client needs an installation of the database vendor's client software and libraries compiled for the client platform. This client software can sometimes be tricky to install. For instance, Oracle client software requires several user environment variables be configured, as well as the editing of system configuration files that point to the host database.

On workstations that make use of multiple database applications, there may end up being multiple versions of the client software installed, sometimes inadvertently and sometimes by necessity.

Support—A Case Scenario

Database user licenses are usually defined in terms of number of concurrent users. So let's say we have a five-user license for your database. First thing in the morning, the users in finance start up their application and start poking around. A user enters some data, and then goes out to lunch, to a meeting, or sits back to read e-mail for an hour. Suddenly, something happens in marketing that requires that department to use the database. They need to update some client information, or perhaps they want to enter a new account into the database.

When they try to connect to the database, they are refused, as the database server knows it already has five active connections ongoing.

Unfortunately, the database server considers an open connection to a client a use of a license. It doesn't matter if the user is completely idle from an application perspective. In fact, to the server, the connection may appear to be active because the vendor protocol layer is always making some demand on it as it makes sure the database is alive and functioning. There's no fix to this. Your user in marketing is locked out until someone else quits the application.

So, the user calls the IT department. They call the DBA. She examines the database to determine who is actively logged in. She calls back the IT support staff and informs them that five users in finance are logged into the database. They call each user to find out who is actively using the application. Finally, they get someone to quit the application. Then the support person calls the user in marketing, and they attempt to log in. I say attempt, because all this time someone else could have also been trying to get in, and managed to do so the very moment the vacancy opened up. In this event, your user in marketing still can't get in, and then starts screaming that the application is junk and you're all incompetent. This is exacerbated by the fact that the user in marketing only needed to make a simple change that should have taken two minutes.

As you can see, both the client and server (and for that matter, user and support staff) waste resources maintaining an unused connection between them. Unused from the point of view of the application, but not from the database. Moreover, since your database is most likely licensed in terms of number of concurrent users, you are now wasting a license that could be used by another application for entering data. Even worse, you may have a situation where everyone in the company needs to enter a small amount of data all at the same time, say 4:30 P.M. You may not only exceed the number of connections your database is allowed to have, but the host machine will thrash unnecessarily trying to open, close, and refuse a large number of concurrent connections. Furthermore, you have a rather inflexible situation that creates a problem for the users, and for the departments that service them. The specialized nature of database application makes it very difficult to educate the users and support staff in this particular problem, and in the end it looks like your fault for putting everyone in this situation.

Come to think of it, maybe it is.

You can solve this problem by buying more licenses, but that's probably a fairly expensive solution. Especially since the system itself is no better for it, and it's probably not in your budget anyway.

Another problem from a software development perspective is that this model forces a fair amount of the application business logic to reside in the client application itself. Because that software may be difficult to deploy, it makes modifications or bug fixes extremely difficult. The turnaround time in just getting a new version of an application installed on a user's workstation can be a frustrating addition to the wait already imposed by the development time. Also, it places additional demands on your IT support staff, who may need to personally visit each machine to install the latest version. Wow, you must be getting very popular by now.

N-tier Model (Three or More Tiers)

In response to these issues, the trend in database computing has been to move to an N-tier solution. In this model, an intermediary or broker machine handles the client requests using a lightweight protocol. These requests are then funneled back to the database using the heavyweight vendor protocol. See Figure 1–2.

Features of the N-tier Model

There are several important features of this model to consider:

Stateless connections between clients and servers. First is the fact that the connection between what the client considers to be the server (now the middle tier) is stateless (it does not remain open). Therefore, during periods of inactivity in the application, neither the client or the server will be using up resources maintaining an unused connection.

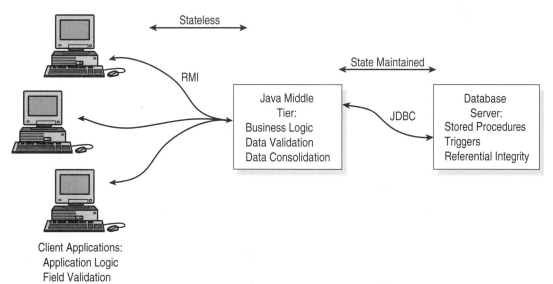

Figure 1–2: N-tier model

No vendor specific protocol is used to communicate between client and server. By brokering the database connection, we can free ourselves from the platform-specific binaries and their complicated installation. Fewer layers on the client side make its operation more stable and easier to debug.

By using Java RMI technology, we can free ourselves from implementing the socket connections, protocols, and other network programming tasks between client and middle tier, thus making development easier.

Connection pooling and load balancing by application type and function is now easily implemented. You can choose to build your middle tier to force multiple clients to share a single, persistent database connection. You can also load balance by having multiple clients share multiple connections, with the connections grouped by application function. For example, you could have a Data Entry object, a Data Validation Object, and a Reporting Object each with their own database connection. A single client could have access to all three objects. Based on the activity in the application, some clients may use only one object and others all three. Lengthy transactions could be queued up to one dedicated object while other objects continue to service requests.

Persistent open database connections between middle tier and database server. Much of the overhead of accessing a database occurs during the initial opening of the connection to the database. By removing this task from the client, initial load times decrease, resulting in perceived performance. The middle tier is ideally a fairly high powered machine with a fast network connection to the database server. The database server now has to manage fewer resources. Since the connection function is now moved to the middle tier, additional performance is gained.

JDBC guarantees database independence. Many database vendors now have Level 4 JDBC drivers available for their database. (A Level 4 driver is a driver that is implemented entirely in Java.) This means your dependence on platform-specific binaries is completely removed. Since the driver is implemented in Java, you can run it—and therefore connect to the database—from any platform. In addition, if you decide to change database vendors, or need to access multiple databases of different vendors from the same middle tier, all you need to do is change your JDBC URLs, and you're ready to go!

JDBC also saves you the task of programming your own database connectivity modules. Furthermore, it is vendor supported, unlike modules you may find to plug into Perl or Python.

Scalability and flexibility. With this design, your system can grow to bridge various data sources, regardless of vendor. Your middle tier could talk to multiple databases of either the same vendor or both. It could also access information from flat files or other network services such as the Web or e-mail.

A More Complex Example of the N-tier Model

Hardware Configuration

In the more complex model shown in Figure 1–3, the database server hardware remains and does not require any change in configuration in order to switch to the N-tier model. In fact, you can continue to provide services to other two-tiered applications simultaneously. The middle tier just becomes another client. Your only issue for the database server will be: does the total number of licenses exceed the existing two-tiered clients, plus the new middle tiers?

Check with your database vendor to make sure your proposed brokering scheme does not conflict with your concurrent users' license. Most database vendors will negotiate a deal for X number of licenses based on proposed application usage.

The middle tier server should be a midsized server, although it all depends on the number of clients you anticipate serving now and in the future. If your budget is small, you could get reasonable performance from a fast workstation class machine. Your budget and support staff will dictate the decision for you, but like your database server, a stable well-supported Unix platform like Solaris will yield the best price performance in the long run.

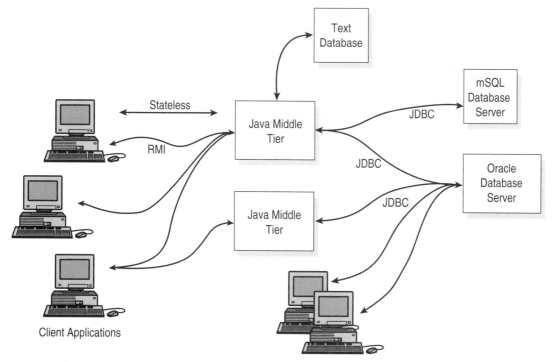

Figure 1–3: A complex example

Network Topology

The middle tier maintains the persistent connection to the database in the same way that the client used to. It manages the connection with the same underlying vendor protocol as your clients. At the same time, it also accepts network connections from client machines in the same way that a Web server would. In fact, many Web servers are used in just this way, to provide public access to some kind of database without each user having direct access to that database. When you browse through the books at Amazon.com, you are accessing their database via a middle tier, their Web server. Not only can you have Web clients access your middle tier, but also it could just as easily be GUI or even command-line clients. In fact, you may even have a Web server access the middle tier as a way of optimizing performance, or you may have both running on the same machine. It all depends on your budget and your needs.

The connections between the clients (whatever they are) and the middle tier are stateless. That is, they only maintain a connection with the middle-tier server long enough to get what they want and then they close the connection. This is exactly what you do when you make a phone call to someone. You call, you chat, and then you hang up. Imagine if you made phone calls in the same way as the two-tiered approach talks to the database. You would call someone, chat for a while, then set the receiver down and go have a sandwich. Maybe an hour later, you might pick up the receiver again and say a few more things, then set the receiver down again. You'd tie up the phone line with all that idle time. You'd never think of doing that with your phone, but lots of folks are content to do that with their database; you shouldn't.

Moreover, you clients no longer communicate with their server (now the middle tier) in a vendor specific protocol. This means several things:

1. The client connection is now lighter, requiring fewer resources to get the same information.

2. The client no longer needs platform-specific drivers, shared objects, or DLLs/DSOs.

Reread those last two points. Consider how much time you or your IT department spends keeping vendor and platform-specific drivers and client software in order. Making sure that the vendor database client-software drivers are loaded properly, in the right place, with the right version, with the user's path and other environment variables set properly, is almost more work than actually developing the application. In addition, the installation and configuration issues usually reflect poorly on your application, even though they aren't your design or fault. This approach throws all that misery in the trash. The only place you need to maintain current vendor-specific drivers is on the middle tier. One machine, that you control.

Administration

From an administration perspective, having an additional server to maintain may seem undesirable. However, the middle tier does not require the same level of expertise to administer as a typical commercial database server does. This machine could be administered by your regular system administrator if need be. In fact, the setup and support of this server is almost exactly like administering a Web server. Fortunately this is a skill that many people are familiar with these days. In later chapters we will take great pains to try to make the administration of the middle tier as similar to a Web server or any generic network service as we can. So while a system administrator or webmaster could take care of your middle tier, it shouldn't be too hard for your DBA to administer it either, if need be.

In addition to acting as the middle tier, you may want to have this server also act as a file/application server, distributing your software via NFS, Samba, HTTP, and FTP. (More on this in Chapter 7.) These are all well-known services and should be within the abilities of a competent system administrator to manage.

Comparing Both Models

There are some things to keep in mind about the two approaches.

It's especially important that when migrating from one model to another you consider the differences in design. The two-tiered model puts all the control in two places at most: the database server and the client. The N-tiered model lets you place control in N places. This is a huge advantage that is often overlooked or misunderstood because of its initial complexity. Again, let's consider the two models from a software perspective.

Application Logic

In Figure 1–4, your application logic will reside in two places only. Your database server—in the form of stored procedures, triggers, and constraints—and your client—in the form of field validation, and other coded business logic.

As you can see in Figure 1–5, in the N-tier model we can control our application logic in a much more flexible manner. We can still have our triggers, procedures, and integrity constraints in the database. Our middle tier can host our business logic in a database-independent way if we wish. Validation can occur not only in the client, but also within the objects we send back and forth to the middle tier to and from the client. And finally, the client can, of course, perform logic specific to that particular application.

There are four advantages to using this model:

1. Potential to access multiple data sources from a single source.

2. Centralized API promotes reuse of database objects.

3. Ability to distribute logic to various components of the system.

4. Reuse of objects to various applications.

Of the many advantages, the greatest is the potential for reuse. By not embedding all the business logic in the client, the middle tier and other objects used by the middle tier can be reused in other applications. Furthermore, as the business rules change, updates can be applied across many applications by updating a single object in the system.

Support

By centralizing your application logic, you should be able to minimize errors through reusing a tested and debugged database application API. Client applications will become simpler in structure and faster to develop.

Configuration and deployment of software is also simplified by centralized administration. This comes at a price, as you have potentially introduced a single point of failure. However, there are other issues to consider regarding inherently distributed applications like database applications:

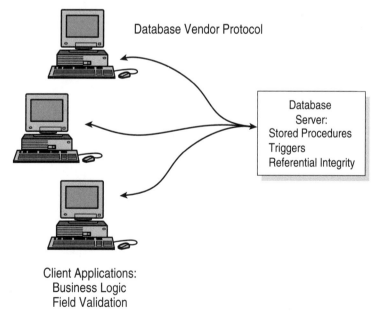

Figure 1–4: Application logic in the two-tier model

1. If your database server is down, your client software is down anyway.

2. If the network is down, your client software is down.

In the N-tier model the following potential problems exist:

1. *Middle tier goes down*. In this instance, you could design the client to failover to another middle-tier server, perhaps running on the database server itself. Or, you could dynamically load code to revert to a two-tier model temporarily.

2. *Database server goes down*. You could design your middle tier to detect the database failure, alert the user, and even allow the user to continue while caching the transactions for later insertion to the database.

3. *Network goes down*. Without the network, none of this works. There's not much you can do about this from a software perspective.

4. *File/Application server goes down*. Clients would have to use an alternative distribution scheme to obtain their software distribution.

Migrating to a Multitier Architecture

The N-tier model has a huge advantage for your database alone; namely, your database no longer has to maintain large numbers of concurrent connections, so your CPU is freed up to do what you want the database to do most—process

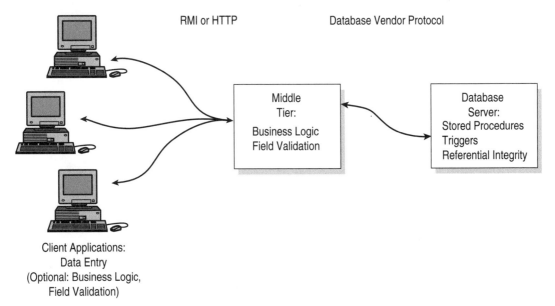

Figure 1–5: Application logic in the N-tier model

queries. Also, by removing all the database connectivity to a middle tier or application server, you can abstract the database into an API for your developers to use. This will speed development in two ways. It will make interaction with the database less error prone, and it will not be necessary for the developer to master SQL, or to embed it into their application.

Migration to a N-tier model does not necessarily require the procurement of additional hardware. There are many ways to reuse existing equipment to build your system. Your system will depend on the number of users you need to support and your desire to scale without additional investment. You may have minimum downtime requirements that would dictate one configuration over another.

Chapter 2

The Database API

Quick Start

Here we introduce the concept of building an API to access a particular Oracle database schema. Pros and cons of various techniques used in database programming are discussed.

The second half of the chapter is devoted to coding an actual API, which will be used throughout the rest of the book in servlets, Swing applications, and command-line clients.

Technology Overview

History of Database Application Programming Techniques

Most database programming is done by embedding SQL statements directly into the application code. While this technique is expedient and pervasive, it often promotes a code maintenance problem as the database schema grows or changes over time. Furthermore, there may occur multiple versions of the same SQL in

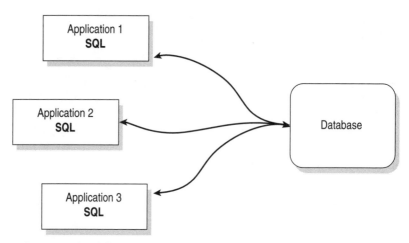

Figure 2–1: Embedding SQL inside application code

various parts of the code, or worse, different SQL statements that produce the same result. This problem only becomes harder to administer as the application grows in scope. It quickly becomes impossible if there are multiple applications that use the same database schema.

Problems with Embedded SQL

As illustrated in Figure 2–1, various applications are written with SQL embedded in their source code. All three applications may contain similar, if not identical, SQL commands. If one application requires a modification of the schema for some reason (the addition of a column in a table, for instance), then all three applications would need to have their source modified and recompiled if they made references to the affected table.

While you can try to build stored procedures in the database to address some of these issues, it still doesn't alleviate the problem when it comes to basic Data Manipulation Language (DML) calls (i.e., INSERT, UPDATE, and DELETE), or even basic Data Query Language (DQL) calls (i.e., SELECT). Furthermore, writing stored procedures requires knowledge of a vendor-specific procedural language (in the case of Oracle, PL/SQL), which may lie outside the skill set of the majority of your development staff (if the feature is available at all in the database you are using).

A Solution with a Database API

Our approach to solving this problem is to build a database API using Java technology. Essentially, this is an effort to abstract the database calls into an API format familiar to a Java programmer. Figure 2–2 shows how the SQL calls (both DML and DQL) are safely tucked away in the implementation code of the API. If for some reason the SQL needs to be modified or optimized, it can be done in one place without negatively impacting the applications that use it. Moreover, all applications that utilize the API can instantly reap the benefits of any improvements to the SQL in the API.

Stored procedures can still be implemented and accessed via the API, so where it makes sense to include them you still can. However, you have the added benefit of allowing your application developers the ability of calling those procedures in the same way they would invoke any Java method call.

To see how this is all implemented, let's start with a practical example by designing a database schema we can use to construct our database API against. After a description of our database schema, we'll build our API with the DML statements first. Then we'll add some common queries (DQL) to the API as well. This will give you a sense of how to handle the basic calls within JDBC and as they relate to RMI. It will also illustrate how you can include other business logic in the methods in an effort to force all your applications to follow certain guidelines by default.

Most of the SQL you'll see in this book will appear in this chapter. Toward that end, I should warn you that the SQL examples are based on Oracle SQL. Oracle's recent port of their server products to Linux creates a unique opportunity for people to take advantage of the many features that a true relational database has to offer on an open source operating system. That's not to say that you can't use another database if you wish. You'll simply have to edit the SQL slightly to conform to either ANSI standard or the form your database prefers.

Most books on database programming build examples based on rather simple, straightforward database schemas. While this promotes quicker understanding

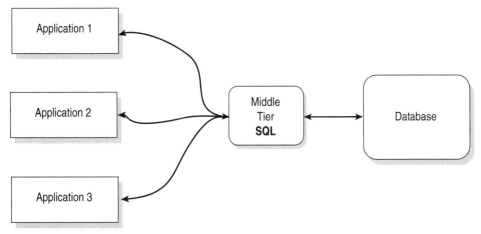

Figure 2–2: Centralizing SQL calls through a database application API

of the topic, it is not always representative of a real-world situation. While I don't want to spend the entire book delving into the intricacies of database schema design, I do want to provide a slightly more complex schema than is usually encountered. In many ways, it will fall short of a real schema, but this will help us illustrate the advantages of building a database API and how Java technology can help you solve some of these problems. If the schema were too simple, it might seem pointless to go to all the work to create a integrated system around it.

An Inventory Database

Our database represents the parts inventory of a less than typical electronics manufacturer. All the parts have some attributes in common, like part number, serial number, weight, color, etc. We will encapsulate these attributes into a table, called UNIT.

The parts have a relationship to each other. One unit may be part of another, larger assembly. The users have decided that what they really want from the system is the ability to easily see these dependencies in the form of a tree. In this way they can quickly generate parts breakdowns from any single point in the assembly.

 NOTE: In a real-world situation, you would of course have a lot more requirements and business logic to deal with. While this may not seem realistic, my explicit goal is to provide just enough complexity so that we can illustrate how to design various parts of the system. In the end, I will have illustrated many reusable pieces of code that address common application development tasks.

```
CREATE TABLE UNIT (
        ID              NUMBER  constraint pk_unit primary key,
        PARENTID        NUMBER,
        NAME            VARCHAR2(30),
        PARTNO          VARCHAR2(10),
        SERIALNO        VARCHAR2(10),
        WEIGHT          NUMBER,
        COLOR           NUMBER,
        MFG             NUMBER,
        CDATE           DATE,
        MDATE           DATE,
        constraint fk_unit foreign key (PARENTID) references UNIT (ID)
)
/
```

```
CREATE TABLE MFG (
        ID                      NUMBER constraint pk_mfg primary key,
        NAME                    VARCHAR2(30)
)
/
CREATE TABLE QTY (
        ID                      NUMBER constraint pk_qty primary key,
        QUANTITY                NUMBER
)
/
CREATE TABLE COLOR (
        ID                      NUMBER constraint pk_color primary key,
        NAME                    VARCHAR2(20)
)
/
```

Schema Design Notes

The UNIT table is joined back upon itself. There is a constraint in the database that forces each record to be parented to another existing record. This creates a one-to-many relationship with itself.

The advantage of this kind of design is that you can have infinite levels of recursion. This enables you to not have to predict all the possibilities up front in your system's analysis phase. You can keep parenting new records as much as you like. For instance, in our example, if you suddenly needed to track another sub-component type, you could without any further modifications to the database. Adding a new level is a built-in feature of the schema, as the ability for records to be parented to new child records can continue infinitely. This kind of design is similar to the file system on a disk, or pages in a book, or many other systems you may have to model that have some kind of hierarchical relationship.

This also makes it trivial to reparent entire family trees. Let's say you needed to transfer an assembly from one product to another. With this design, all you would have to do is change the parentseq from one ID to another and all the relationships would be maintained.

However, there is also more than one drawback to this kind of schema, namely that ad-hoc querying becomes only possible by professional database programmers. There may also be performance implications in report generation as well. The SQL used to do the queries may need to be carefully tuned, or multiple selects may be required in order to obtain the needed data for the report. In many situations, this kind of schema design would have a steep learning curve for most developers. However, by having our database API, once the SQL is crafted by your top SQL guru, the rest of the development team need not worry about it and simply make use of the API.

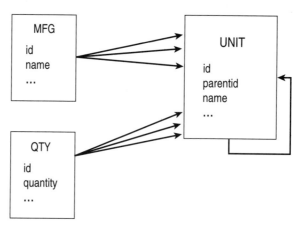

Figure 2–3: Database schema for inventory database

Finally, in a more traditional one-to-many relationship, tables for the manufacturer name and quantity are foreign-key linked back to the unit table, as shown in Figure 2–3.

The biggest point to understand for our purposes is that no matter what your schema, you can abstract that via a database API in order to make it more accessible to your application programmers. You can also flatten out these complex relationships into method calls that return just what the application developer wants.

API Design

Overview

The API will be an object that does the following for us:

1. Implements our database application access.

2. Provides some application-wide business logic.

3. Manages our database connection.

We'll be using RMI Java technology to communicate between our clients and our Database API. If you don't already understand the basics of RMI, let's do a quick overview.

RMI

Remote Method Invocation (RMI) is a set of APIs in the core Java implementation. It enables you to access Java objects remotely without having to actually code the network connection and protocols yourself. On the server side, you publish an object by giving it a name in a registry (more about this in Chapter 3) and creating an instance of it. Then you give your client a URL where that object lives. The client accesses the registry to see if the object exists. If it finds it, it uses an outline of the class (Stub) that provides the client with enough information about the class to know what the callable methods and return types are.

Once the client has a handle or reference to the remote object, it proceeds to call the methods of that object as if it were local. No special network calls are made by the application programmer. RMI handles that dynamically for you.

This is our key to making the client independent from the database. By using RMI, a core feature of the Java runtime environment, we no longer require any third-party drivers to talk to our database. Our middle tier brokers the connection for us by using JDBC on one side to the database, and RMI to the clients. Since RMI is a feature of any 1.1 compliant JRE or JDK, we have no additional software to distribute beyond our own code and the JRE itself.

RMI is an excellent way for you to make available tools and systems to other platforms. By building RMI implementations that wrap systems available on the RMI server host, you can make accessible tools and software that might not be otherwise accessible.

Identifying Your Database Needs by Building an Interface

The first step in building an RMI object is to define an interface object that extends java.rmi.Remote. This is a necessary step in building RMI applications, and it's also a great way to plan out your needs for the database API while simultaneously implementing it.

An interface is a object that defines a guaranteed set of functionality for any object that implements it. The actual methods of an interface have no code in them. They are just there to provide a known framework that other developers can build on without being concerned about the implementation. When you actually implement the interface, the compiler makes sure that you have implemented all the methods of the interface by checking your code against them.

Using this kind of framework makes it easy for you to build new implementations of the interface without breaking existing applications. Since the applications only know of the interface, if you change the implementation details (such as what database you're using), or alter the underlying business logic, your applications will still function. This gives you a built-in strategy for ongoing software modification as the needs of the business change without having to constantly rebuild from scratch.

In our application, we know that we will need to modify the UNIT table. So, our interface defines the following methods:

```
public interface UnitDb extends Remote {
    public int insertUnit(UnitInfo u) throws RemoteException;
    public void updateUnit(UnitInfo u) throws RemoteException;
    public void deleteUnit(int u) throws RemoteException;
```

These three methods provide us with standard DML access to the UNIT table. In order to easily pass along all the information that we may need to provide to the database in one variable, we have built a serialized object called UnitInfo that represents the structure of the database table, plus some error handling.

Representing Database Tables with Serialized Objects

Here we take the contents of the database table we're interested in modifying and turn it into an object we can pass back and forth across the network or save out to the file system. We do this by having the object implement the serializable interface from the java.io package.

The object looks something like this (a complete listing of this object is at the end of the chapter):

```java
import java.io.*;
import java.util.Date;

public class UnitInfo implements Serializable {

    public UnitInfo() {

    }

    /**
     * This constructor can be used to quickly populate a
     *   UnitInfo object. Quick only in the sense that you can
     *   build it all on one line. WARNING: using this
     *   constructor bypasses the validation logic, so use with
     *   care. This constructor can be useful when populating
     *   directly from the database, where the data is
     *   hopefully already validated.
     */
    public UnitInfo(int i, int p, String n, String pn,
                    String sn, float w, int c, int m,
                    Date cd, Date md) {
        id = i;
        parentid = p;
        name = n;
        partno = pn;
        serialno = sn;
        weight = w;
        colorid = c;
        mfgid = m;
        cdate = cd;
        mdate = md;

    }
```

```
    int id;

    /**
     * Get the value of id, the primary database key for the UNIT
     * table. @return Value of id.
     */
    public int getId() {return id;}

    /**
     * Set the value of id, the primary key for this entity.
     * @param v  Value to assign to id.
     */
    public void setId(int   v) {this.id = v;}

    int parentid;

    /**
     * Get the value of parentid, the key (ID) of the record in the
     * database that this entity is a child of. if no parent is set,
     *  it will assume the root parent ( 0 ). if you wanted to make
     *  sure that the parentid was set by the application, you could
     *  make this object set it to -1 when instantiated and then test
     *  for that value in your application code. Even if you forget to
     *  test, Oracle will throw a SqlException from encountering an
     *  integrity constraint. As long as you haven't already inserted a
     * record with -1 as the ID, that is! @return Value of parentid.
     */
    public int getParentid() {
       return parentid;
    }

    /**
     * Set the value of parentid.
     * @param v  Value to assign to parentid.
     */
    public void setParentid(int   v) {this.parentid = v;}

    String name;

    /**
     * Get the unit name.
     * @return UNIT name.
     */
    public String getName() {return name;}
```

```
/**
 * Set the value of the UNIT name.
 * @param v  Value to assign to UNIT name.
 */
public void setName(String  v) {this.name = v;}




        .

        .

        .

        .



float weight;

/**
 * Get the UNIT weight.
 * @return Value of weight.
 */
public float getWeight() {return weight;}

/**
 * Set the UNIT weight.
 * @param v  Value to assign to weight.
 */
/* public void setWeight(float  v) {this.weight = v;} */

public void setWeight(float f) throws BadWeightException {
   if (f <= 0.0) {
       BadWeightException b = new BadWeightException();
       throw b;
   }
   else {
       weight = f;
   }
}



     .

     .

     .

     .



/**
 * This is a method you can use to quickly view the object's
 *  contents. You may want to override this if you want to use
 *  this object in a GUI control or widget.
 *
 *  In this form, you can just do:
 *  System.out.println(unitinfo);
 *  ...and get a nice listing of the object values.
```

```
 *
 * @param nil a value of type ''
 * @return a value of type 'String'
 */
public String toString() {
    String s = "id: " + getId() + "\n" +
        "name: " + getName() + "\n" +
        "parentid:" + getParentid() + "\n" +
        "partno: " + getPartno() + "\n" +
        "serialno: " + getSerialno() + "\n" +
        "weight: " + getWeight() + "\n" +
        "colorid: " + getColorid() + "\n" +
        "mfgid: " + getMfgid() + "\n" +
        "cdate: " + getCdate() + "\n" +
        "mdate: " + getMdate() + "\n" +
        "parentname: " + getParentname() + "\n";
    return s;
}

} // UnitInfo
```

Each column in the database table UNIT is represented by a global variable of the correct type, as well as having corresponding set and get methods. This immediately provides one level of validation by not being able to pass a string into the setWeight() method. You could also add additional code to do more complete data validation. For instance, let's say that you wanted to make sure that no new entries went in to the database unless the weight was greater than zero. You could rewrite the setWeight() method as follows:

```
public void setWeight(float f) throws BadWeightException {
    if (f !> 0.0) {
        BadWeightException b = new BadWeightException();
        throw b;
    }
    else {
        weight = f;
    }
}

public class BadWeightException extends Exception {};
```

Likewise, you could also do other types of data validation here, making sure values are in a certain range, that strings are all converted to upper or lower case, whatever is necessary to your application. You may have already placed constraints on your database table to enforce these values, but this enables your client applications to enforce the rules before they try to access the database. In this way you can improve performance and responsiveness of your application by being able to catch common errors before they make the trip all the way to the database.

Also note the use of comments. This commenting style makes use of javadoc syntax, which lets you take advantage of the automatic HTML documentation generator provided as a part of the JDK. You'll find this kind of syntax very valuable in providing immediate documentation of your classes. The latest version of javadoc that comes with Java 2 makes particularly attractive HTML documents. See Appendix A to view the generated HTML API documentation of the examples in this book.

Retrieving Data from the API

Now that we have a means of modifying the database, we need to define some methods to get information out. One of the things we'll want to do is to view the data in a hierarchial format. It's our intention to be able to browse the data using the Swing JTree component. In order to help us implement this later, we'll define the following method.

```
/**
 *   getChildUnits is used to find all the units that are
 *   directly parented to the unit whose key is passed in.
 *   This method is particularly useful for trees.
 *
 *   @param u a value of type 'int', the parent key.
 *   @return a value of type 'Vector' containing UnitInfo
 *   objects @exception RemoteException if an error occurs
 */
public Vector getChildUnits(int u)  throws RemoteException;
```

Next we'll need a method to get a complete record from the UNIT table for either examination or editing purposes.

```
/**
 *   getUnitInfo returns a complete UnitInfo object given
 *   that object's key.
 *
 *   @param u a value of type 'int'
 *   @return a value of type 'UnitInfo'
 *   @exception RemoteException if an error occurs
 */
public UnitInfo getUnitInfo(int u) throws RemoteException;
```

This method will work well in situations where we already know the unique ID for the record we want (such as browsing a tree), but for instances where we need to search for something, we'll need to define a more traditional search method.

```
/**
 * findUnit returns a hashtable of matches, key being a
 *  String of matching text and value being the database
 *  key for corresponding UnitInfo object.
 *
 * @param s a value of type 'String'
 * @return a value of type 'Hashtable'
 * @exception RemoteException if an error occurs
 */
public Hashtable findUnit(String s) throws RemoteException;
```

This method does not return the UnitInfo object directly, but rather returns a HashTable object containing the matched string and a corresponding ID key. This can be easily passed into a JList or other choosing component for the user to select the correct match. (More on this in Chapter 4). The selection can be bound to a listener that then retrieves the correct UnitInfo object from the database (by calling getUnitInfo()).

That concludes our interface for now. The next step is to build a implementation of this interface that actually makes the database connection, and retrieves the data from the database.

The Implementation

As stated before, we need to implement all the methods in our interface in order to conform to that specification. However, we're going to need to add a few additional methods as well. The first one will be in actually connecting to the database.

Connecting to Oracle via JDBC

```
public class UnitDbImpl extends UnicastRemoteObject implements UnitDb {
```

Extending the UnicastRemoteObject is required in order to use RMI. At this point that's all you need to know about that. We implement our database interface, our promise to provide working versions of those methods.

```
private Connection conn;
private String url, user, pass, instance, hostname;
```

We make the connection object global so that we can access it from the various methods of the class. Also, we want to keep that connection open over the life of the class. The strings are for use in connecting to the database, stored globally for convenience and in case we have to reconnect to the database.

```
public static final int DB_DOWN = 0;
public static final int LSNR_DOWN = 1034;
```

These values are the error codes Oracle's JDBC driver returns for the database being down or the SQLNet listener being down. We state these here for convenience in our error handling later.

```
public UnitDbImpl() throws RemoteException {
   // set the defaults
   hostname = "localhost";
   instance = "UNIT";
   user = "unit";
   pass = "pass";

   try {
       Class.forName ("oracle.jdbc.driver.OracleDriver");
       url = "jdbc:oracle:thin:@" + hostname + ":1521:" + instance;
       conn = DriverManager.getConnection (url, user, pass);
   }
   catch (ClassNotFoundException ce) {
       RemoteException re = new RemoteException(ce.getMessage());
       throw re;
   }
   catch (SQLException se) {
       RemoteException re = new RemoteException(ce.getMessage());
       throw re;
   }
}
```

Here is our first constructor. We take in no parameters and hard code default values for the database location, username, and password. Obviously, you may not wish to only have a default constructor with hardcoded passwords.

```
public UnitDbImpl(String user, String pass, String hostname,
                  String instance) throws RemoteException {
       try {
           Class.forName ("oracle.jdbc.driver.OracleDriver");
           url = "jdbc:oracle:thin:@" + hostname + ":1521:" + instance;
           conn = DriverManager.getConnection (url, user, pass);
       }
       catch (ClassNotFoundException ce) {
           RemoteException re = new RemoteException(ce.getMessage());
           throw re;
       }
       catch (SQLException se) {
           RemoteException re = new RemoteException(ce.getMessage());
           throw re;
       }
}
```

The second constructor allows us to pass in whatever values we desire so that we can control all parameters of the database login. We can change the instance and host easily for testing against a development instance or if the database server is replaced later.

In designing our object we want to have the most flexibility possible as far as the ability to connect to the database. A typical JDBC URL for Oracle looks like this:

```
String dburl = "jdbc:oracle:thin:@hostname:1521:instance";
```

The database connection is actually opened by:

```
conn = DriverManager.getConnection (dburl, user, pass);
```

So, the most flexible thing to do is to have two constructors: one that assumes whatever default values you want, and one that lets you specify all the variables.

Conclusion

Although it may not seem so right now, we've accomplished a lot. More important, we now have a generalized, accessible way for developers to interact with our database schema. Even better, we have a reusable object that will find its way into a wide variety of applications that previously would have all been hard coded with similar SQL calls to the database. In the following chapters, we will take this API and use it in a lightweight GUI swing client, a command-line utility, and a Web application.

Complete Code Listings

Listing 2–1: UnitDb.java

```java
import java.util.*;
import java.rmi.*;
import java.awt.*;
import java.io.*;

/**
 *  The UnitDB Interface. This is the template that we build the database
 *  API from. Notice that in this class we do not worry about the JDBC-
 *  specific elements. Only the application-specific elements are defined.
 *
 * @author (c)1999, 2000 Stewart Birnam
 * @version 1.0
 */
public interface UnitDb extends Remote {

        /*-------------------------------------------------------------*
         *  DML methods
         *  these methods provide the basic insert, update and delete methods.
         *  they make use of a UnitInfo entity object, which is s Serialized
         *  Java object that contains all the information necessary for making
```

```
 *   any kind of change to the database.
 *------------------------------------------------------------------*/

public int insertUnit(UnitInfo u) throws RemoteException;

public void updateUnit(UnitInfo u) throws RemoteException;

public void deleteUnit(int u) throws RemoteException;

/*------------------------------------------------------------------*
 *   DQL methods
 *------------------------------------------------------------------*/

/**
 *   getChildUnits is used to find all the units that are directly
 *   parented to the unit whose key is passed in. This method is
 *   particularly useful for trees.
 *
 * @param u a value of type 'int', the parent key.
 * @return a value of type 'Vector' containing UnitInfo objects
 * @exception RemoteException if an error occurs
 */
public Vector getChildUnits(int u)   throws RemoteException;

/**
 *   getUnitInfo returns a complete UnitInfo object given that
 *   object's key.
 *
 * @param u a value of type 'int'
 * @return a value of type 'UnitInfo'
 * @exception RemoteException if an error occurs
 */
public UnitInfo getUnitInfo(int u) throws RemoteException;

/**
 * getMfg returns a hashtable containing a key/value pair
 *  with the key being a String (manufacturer name) and the
 *  value being an Integer (manufacturer database key).
 *
 * @return a value of type 'Hashtable'
 * @exception RemoteException if an error occurs
 */
public Hashtable getMfg() throws RemoteException;

/**
 * getColor returns a hashtable with the key being the
 *  color name (String) and the value being the
 *  database key
```

```
     *
     * @param nil a value of type ''
     * @return a value of type 'Hashtable'
     * @exception RemoteException if an error occurs
     */
    public Hashtable getColor() throws RemoteException;

    /**
     * findUnit returns a hashtable of matches, key being a String
     *   of matching text and value being the database key for
     *   corresponding UnitInfo object.
     *
     * @param s a value of type 'String'
     * @return a value of type 'Hashtable'
     * @exception RemoteException if an error occurs
     */
    public Hashtable findUnit(String s) throws RemoteException;

    /**
     * findColor returns a Vector of UnitInfo objects that match the
     * color name passed in.
     *
     * @param s a value of type 'String'
     * @return a value of type 'Vector'
     * @exception RemoteException if an error occurs
     */
    public Vector findColor(String s) throws RemoteException;
}
```

Listing 2–2: UnitDbImpl.java

```
import java.sql.*;
import oracle.*;
import java.util.*;
import java.rmi.*;
import java.rmi.server.*;
import java.text.*;
import java.util.Date;
import java.io.*;


/**
 * UnitDbImpl.java
 *
 *
 * Created: Wed Dec 29 22:58:15 1999
 *
 * @author (c) 1999, 2000 Stewart Birnam
 * @version 1.0
 */
```

```
public class UnitDbImpl extends UnicastRemoteObject implements UnitDb {

    private Connection conn; // our connection to the database
    private String url, user, pass, instance, hostname;

    // these values are the SQL error codes from an ORACLE database
    // DB_DOWN is the error code you receive when you can't connect to
    // the database LSNR_DOWN is the error code you get when the Oracle
    // Listener is down.
    public static final int DB_DOWN = 0;
    public static final int LSNR_DOWN = 1034;

    // we'll use this for converting Dates to the string Oracle wants
    // to see. Take a look at oraDate in the DbUtil class below.
    public SimpleDateFormat formatter
        = new SimpleDateFormat("MM/dd/yyyy HH:mm");

    public UnitDbImpl() throws RemoteException {
        // set the defaults
        hostname = "localhost";
        instance = "book";
        user = "stewartb";
        pass = "stewartb";

        try {
            Class.forName ("oracle.jdbc.driver.OracleDriver");
            url = "jdbc:oracle:thin:@" + hostname + ":1521:" + instance;
            conn = DriverManager.getConnection (url, user, pass);
            // you can use these two lines instead
            // if you're trying to use
            // this with personal oracle lite for win98/95
            //Class.forName("oracle.lite.poljdbc.POLJDBCDriver");
            //conn = DriverManager.getConnection("jdbc:polite:POLITE",
            //                                    "scott", "tiger");

        }
        catch (ClassNotFoundException ce) {
            RemoteException re = new RemoteException(ce.getMessage());
            throw re;
        }
        catch (SQLException se) {
            RemoteException re = new RemoteException(se.getMessage());
            throw re;
        }
    }
}
```

```java
public UnitDbImpl(String user, String pass, String hostname,
                  String instance) throws RemoteException {
    try {
        Class.forName ("oracle.jdbc.driver.OracleDriver");
        url = "jdbc:oracle:thin:@" + hostname + ":1521:" + instance;
        conn = DriverManager.getConnection (url, user, pass);
    }
    catch (ClassNotFoundException ce) {
        RemoteException re = new RemoteException(ce.getMessage());
        throw re;
    }
    catch (SQLException se) {
        RemoteException re = new RemoteException(se.getMessage());
        throw re;
    }
}


public synchronized int insertUnit(UnitInfo u) throws RemoteException {
    int newid = -1;
    int response;
    try {
        newid = this.getNextSeq();
        String sql =  "insert into UNIT " +
            "(id, parentid, name, partno, " +
            "serialno, weight, color, mfg, " +
            "cdate, mdate) " +
            "values ( " +
            newid + ", " +
            u.getParentid() + ", " +
            DbUtil.oraParse(u.getName()) + ", " +
            DbUtil.oraParse(u.getPartno()) + ", " +
            DbUtil.oraParse(u.getSerialno()) + ", " +
            u.getWeight() + ", " +
            u.getColorid() + ", " +
            u.getMfgid() + ", " +
            "SYSDATE, " +
            "SYSDATE )";

        Statement stmt = conn.createStatement();
        response = stmt.executeUpdate(sql);
        conn.commit();
        stmt.close();

    }
```

```
        catch (SQLException se) {
            RemoteException re = new RemoteException(se.getMessage());
                throw re;
        }
        return newid;
    }


    public synchronized void updateUnit(UnitInfo u) throws RemoteException {
        int response;
        try {
            String sql =   "update UNIT set " +
            "parentid = " + u.getParentid() + ", " +
            "name = " + DbUtil.oraParse(u.getName()) + ", " +
            "partno = " + DbUtil.oraParse(u.getPartno()) + ", " +
            "serialno = " + DbUtil.oraParse(u.getSerialno()) + ", " +
            "weight = " + u.getWeight() + ", " +
            "color = " + u.getColorid() + ", " +
            "mfg = " + u.getMfgid() + ", " +
            "mdate = SYSDATE " +
            "where id = " + u.getId();

            Statement stmt = conn.createStatement();
            response = stmt.executeUpdate(sql);
            conn.commit();
            stmt.close();


        }
        catch (SQLException se) {
            RemoteException re = new RemoteException(se.getMessage());
            throw re;
        }
    }


    public synchronized void deleteUnit(int i) throws RemoteException {
        int response;
        try {
            String sql = "delete from UNIT where id = " + i;
            Statement stmt = conn.createStatement();
            response = stmt.executeUpdate(sql);
            conn.commit();
            stmt.close();
        }
        catch (SQLException se) {
            RemoteException re = new RemoteException(se.getMessage());
            throw re;
        }
    }
```

```java
/**
 * getChildUnits returns a vector of UnitNode objects. These are
 * stipped down versions of the UnitInfo object, containing just what
 *  is needed in a tree situation. This helps keep the potential
 *  transfer of large numbers of records fast.
 *
 * @param u a value of type 'int'
 * @return a value of type 'Vector'
 * @exception RemoteException if an error occurs
 */
public synchronized Vector getChildUnits(int u)
    throws RemoteException {
    Vector v = new Vector();
    String sql = "select child.id, child.parentid, child.name, " +
        "parent.name from unit child, unit parent " +
        "where child.id != 0 and " +
        "child.parentid = parent.id and " +
        "child.parentid = " + u + " order by child.name";
    try {
        Statement stmt = conn.createStatement();
        ResultSet rs = stmt.executeQuery(sql);
        if ( rs.next() == false ) {
            rs.close();
            stmt.close();
        } else {

            do {
                UnitNode un = new UnitNode(rs.getInt(1),
                        rs.getInt(2), rs.getString(3));
                un.setParentname(rs.getString(4));
                v.addElement(un);
            }
            while (rs.next());

            rs.close();
            stmt.close();
        }
    }
    catch (SQLException e) {
        RemoteException re = new RemoteException(e.getMessage() +
            "\n" + sql );
        throw re;
    }

    return v;
}
```

```
public synchronized UnitInfo getUnitInfo(int u)
    throws RemoteException {
    UnitInfo unitinfo = new UnitInfo();
    String sql = "select child.id, child.parentid, " +
                 "child.name, child.partno, child.serialno, " +
                 "child.weight, child.color, child.mfg, child.mdate, " +
                 "child.cdate, parent.name " +
                 "from unit child, unit parent " +
                 "where child.id = " + u + " and " +
                 "child.parentid = parent.id";
    try {
        Statement stmt = conn.createStatement();
        ResultSet rs = stmt.executeQuery(sql);
        if ( rs.next() == false ) {
            rs.close();
            stmt.close();
        } else {

            do {
                unitinfo = new UnitInfo(rs.getInt(1), rs.getInt(2),
                                    rs.getString(3),rs.getString(4),
                                    rs.getString(5),rs.getFloat(6),
                                    rs.getInt(7), rs.getInt(8),
                                    rs.getDate(9), rs.getDate(10));
                unitinfo.setParentname(rs.getString(11));
            }
            while (rs.next()) ;

            rs.close();
            stmt.close();
        }
    }
    catch (SQLException e) {
        RemoteException re = new RemoteException(e.getMessage() + "\n" + sql);
        throw re;
    }
    return unitinfo;
}

public synchronized Hashtable getMfg() throws RemoteException {
    Hashtable h = new Hashtable();
    String sql = "select id, name from mfg";
    try {
        Statement stmt = conn.createStatement();
        ResultSet rs = stmt.executeQuery(sql);
        if ( rs.next() == false ) {
            rs.close();
            stmt.close();
        } else {
```

```
            // key is the String so that you can use keys() to retrieve
            // a list for a JList or JComboBox, and then use the user
            // selected String to find the database key from the hash.
            do {
                h.put(rs.getString(2), new Integer(rs.getInt(1)));
            }
            while (rs.next()) ;

            rs.close();
            stmt.close();
        }
    }
    catch (SQLException e) {
        RemoteException re = new RemoteException(e.getMessage());
        throw re;
    }
    return h;
}

public synchronized Hashtable getColor() throws RemoteException {
    Hashtable h = new Hashtable();
    String sql = "select id, name from color";
    try {
        Statement stmt = conn.createStatement();
        ResultSet rs = stmt.executeQuery(sql);
        if ( rs.next() == false ) {
            rs.close();
            stmt.close();
        } else {
        // key is the String so that you can use keys() to retrieve
        // a list for a JList or JComboBox, and then use the user
        // selected String to find the database key from the hash.
            do {
                h.put(rs.getString(2), new Integer(rs.getInt(1)));
            }
            while (rs.next()) ;

            rs.close();
            stmt.close();
        }
    }
    catch (SQLException e) {
        RemoteException re = new RemoteException(e.getMessage());
        throw re;
    }
    return h;
}
```

```java
public synchronized Hashtable findUnit(String s)
    throws RemoteException {
    Hashtable h = new Hashtable();
    String sql = "select id, name " +
                "from unit where lower(name) like " +
                DbUtil.oraParse(s + "%").toLowerCase();
    try {
        Statement stmt = conn.createStatement();
        ResultSet rs = stmt.executeQuery(sql);
        if ( rs.next() == false ) {
            rs.close();
            stmt.close();
        } else {
            do {
                h.put(rs.getString(2), new Integer(rs.getInt(1)));
            }
            while (rs.next()) ;

            rs.close();
            stmt.close();
        }
    }
    catch (SQLException e) {
        RemoteException re = new RemoteException(e.getMessage());
        throw re;
    }
    return h;
}

public Vector findColor(String s) throws RemoteException {
    Vector v = new Vector();
    UnitInfo unitinfo;
    String sql = "select unit.id, unit.parentid, unit.name," +
                "unit.partno, unit.serialno, " +
                "unit.weight, unit.color, unit.mfg, unit.mdate, unit.cdate " +
                "from unit, color " +
                "where unit.color = color.id and " +
                "lower(color.name) = " + DbUtil.oraParse(s).toLowerCase();



    try {
        Statement stmt = conn.createStatement();
        ResultSet rs = stmt.executeQuery(sql);
        if ( rs.next() == false ) {
            rs.close();
            stmt.close();
        } else {
```

```
            do {
                unitinfo = new UnitInfo(rs.getInt(1),
                            rs.getInt(2), rs.getString(3),
                            rs.getString(4), rs.getString(5),
                            rs.getFloat(6), rs.getInt(7), rs.getInt(8),
                            rs.getDate(9), rs.getDate(10));
                            v.addElement(unitinfo);
            }
            while (rs.next()) ;

                rs.close();
                stmt.close();
            }
    }
    catch (SQLException e) {
        RemoteException re = new RemoteException(e.getMessage());
        throw re;
    }
    return v;

}


/*--------------------------------*
 *  BLOB - Image handling routines
 *--------------------------------*/

public synchronized InputStream getUnitImage(int u)
            throws RemoteException {

    InputStream is = null;

    String sql = "select image from image where id = " + u;

    try {

        Statement stmt = conn.createStatement();
        ResultSet rs = stmt.executeQuery(sql);

        if ( rs.next()) {
            is = rs.getBinaryStream(1);
        }

        rs.close();
        stmt.close();
    }
    catch (Exception e){
        System.out.println(sql);
        e.printStackTrace();
    }

    return is;

}
```

```
public synchronized int insertImageMetaData(int unitid, int formatid)
        throws RemoteException {
    int imageid = -1;
    String sql = new String();
    try {
        imageid = getNextSeq();
        sql = "insert into image (id, unitid, format) values ( " +
                imageid + ", " + unitid + ", " + formatid + ")";
        Statement stmt = conn.createStatement();
        stmt.execute(sql);
        stmt.close();
    }
    catch (Exception e){
        RemoteException re = new RemoteException(sql + "\n" +
                                                e.getMessage());
        throw re;
    }

    return imageid;
}

public synchronized void updateImage(ByteArrayInputStream b,
                            int size, int imageid)
                            throws RemoteException {
    try {
        PreparedStatement pstmt =
            conn.prepareStatement(
                "update image set image = ? where id = ?" );
        pstmt.setBinaryStream (1, b, size);
        pstmt.setInt( 2,   imageid );

        pstmt.execute ();
        pstmt.close();
    }
    catch (SQLException se) {
        RemoteException re = new RemoteException(se.getMessage());
        throw re;
    }
}

public synchronized Hashtable getImageType() throws RemoteException {
    Hashtable h = new Hashtable();
    String sql = "select id, name from imageformat";
    try {
        Statement stmt = conn.createStatement();
        ResultSet rs = stmt.executeQuery(sql);
        if ( rs.next() == false ) {
            rs.close();
            stmt.close();
        } else {
            do {
                h.put(rs.getString(2), new Integer(rs.getInt(1)));
            }
```

```
            while (rs.next()) ;

            rs.close();
            stmt.close();
        }
    }
    catch (SQLException e) {
        RemoteException re = new RemoteException(e.getMessage());
        throw re;
    }
    return h;
}

public synchronized int insertImageType(String s)
    throws RemoteException {
    int imagetypeid = -1;
    try {
        imagetypeid = getNextSeq();
        String sql = "insert into imageformat (id, name) values ( " +
                        imagetypeid + ", " +  DbUtil.oraParse(s) + ")";
        Statement stmt = conn.createStatement();
        stmt.execute(sql);
        stmt.close();
    }
    catch (Exception e) {
        RemoteException re = new RemoteException(e.getMessage());
        throw re;
    }
    return imagetypeid;
}

/**
 *   convenience method to return the next value from an Oracle Sequence
 *   object. if using another database, you could define
 *   some unique id number generator here.
 *
 * @return a value of type 'int'
 * @exception SQLException if an error occurs
 */
public synchronized int getNextSeq() throws SQLException {
    int seq = -1;
    String sql = "SELECT unitseq.nextval FROM dual";
    try {
        Statement stmt = conn.createStatement();
        ResultSet rs = stmt.executeQuery(sql);
        if ( rs.next() == false ) {
            rs.close();
            stmt.close();
        } else {

            do {
                seq = rs.getInt(1);
            }
```

```
                while (rs.next()) ;

                rs.close();
                stmt.close();
            }
        }
        catch (SQLException e) {
            throw e;
        }
        return seq;
    }

    public synchronized static void main(String[] args) {
        // test the class before deploying

        try {
            UnitDbImpl u = new UnitDbImpl();
            UnitInfo unitinfo = new UnitInfo(1,0,"foo","1234W","ZZZ44",
                                    6.7f, 1, 1, new Date(), new Date());
            System.out.println(unitinfo);
            int id = u.insertUnit(unitinfo);
            System.out.println("id:" + id);
            unitinfo = u.getUnitInfo(id);
            System.out.println(unitinfo);

        }
        catch (RemoteException r) {
            r.printStackTrace();
        }
        System.exit(0);
    }
}
```

Listing 2–3: DbUtil.java

```
class DbUtil {
    public SimpleDateFormat formatter
    = new SimpleDateFormat ("MM/dd/yyyy HH:mm");

    public static String parse (String s, String d) {
     StringTokenizer st = new StringTokenizer(s, d);
     String fixed = new String("");
     while (st.hasMoreTokens()) {
         if (fixed.equals("")) {
           fixed = st.nextToken();
         } else {
           fixed = fixed + d + d + st.nextToken();
         }
     }
```

```java
    if (s.indexOf(d) == 0) {
        fixed = d + d + fixed;
    }


    if (s.lastIndexOf(d) == (s.length() - 1) ){
        fixed = fixed + d + d;
    }

    return fixed;
    }

/**
 * oraParse returns a String bound with single quotes and
 *  with any single quote that may appear in the String
 *  doubled. This makes it ready for insertion into a
 *  oracle database.
 *
 * @param s a value of type 'String' example: Alice's Restaurant
 * @return a value of type 'String'  example: 'Alice''s Restaurant'
 */
public synchronized static String oraParse(String s) {
    if (s == null) { return new String (""); }
    if (s.equals("") || s.equals("null")) { return new String (""); }
    String fixed = new String("");
    fixed = parse(s, "'");
    fixed = "'" + fixed + "'";
    return fixed;
}


/**
 * oraDate like oraParse saves us some typing by converting a
 * java.Date object into the format Oracle wants when inserting .
 * records
 * @param d a value of type 'Date'
 * @return a value of type 'String'
 */
public synchronized String oraDate(Date d)  {
    if (d != null) {
      return "to_date('" + formatter.format(d) +
                    "', 'MM/DD/YYYY HH24:MI')";
    } else {
      return "'";
    }
  }
}
```

Listing 2–4: UnitInfo.java

```java
import java.io.*;
import java.util.Date;
/**
 * UnitInfo.java
 *
 *
 * Created: Thu Sep 23 23:08:27 1999
 *
 * @author (c) 1999, 2000 Stewart Birnam
 * @version 1.0
 */

public class UnitInfo implements Serializable {

    public UnitInfo() {
    }

    /**
     * This constructor can be used to quickly
     * populate a UnitInfo object.
     *  Quick only in the sense that you can build it all on one line.
     *  WARNING: using this constructor bypasses the validation logic, so
     *  use with care. This constructor can be useful when populating
     *  directly from the database, where the data is hopefully already
     *  validated.
     * @param id a value of type 'int'
     * @param parentid a value of type 'int'
     * @param name a value of type 'String'
     * @param partno a value of type 'String'
     * @param serialno a value of type 'String'
     * @param weight a value of type 'float'
     * @param colorid a value of type 'int'
     * @param mfgid a value of type 'int'
     * @param creationDate a value of type 'Date'
     * @param modificationDate a value of type 'Date'
     */
    public UnitInfo(int i, int p, String n, String pn, String sn,
                    float w, int c, int m,
                    Date cd, Date md) {
        id = i;
        parentid = p;
        name = n;
        partno = pn;
        serialno = sn;
        weight = w;
```

```
        colorid = c;
        mfgid = m;
        cdate = cd;
        mdate = md;

}

int id;

/**
 * Get the value of id, the primary database key for the UNIT table.
 * @return Value of id.
 */
public int getId() {return id;}

/**
 * Set the value of id, the primary key for this entity.
 * @param v  Value to assign to id.
 */
public void setId(int  v) {this.id = v;}

int parentid;

/**
 * Get the value of parentid, the key (ID) of the record in the
 * database that this entity is a child of. if no parent is set, it
 *  will assume the root parent ( 0 ). if you wanted to make sure
 *  that the parentid was set by the application, you could make this
 *  object set it to -1 when instantiated and then test for that
 *  value in your application code. Even if you forget to test,
 *  Oracle will throw a SqlException from encountering an integrity
 *  constraint. As long as you haven't already inserted a record with
 *  -1 as the ID, that is!
 * @return Value of parentid.
 */
public int getParentid() {
    return parentid;
}

/**
 * Set the value of parentid.
 * @param v  Value to assign to parentid.
 */
public void setParentid(int  v) {this.parentid = v;}

String name;
```

```java
/**
 * Get the unit name.
 * @return UNIT name.
 */
public String getName() {return name;}

/**
 * Set the value of the UNIT name.
 * @param v  Value to assign to UNIT name.
 */
public void setName(String  v) {this.name = v;}

String partno;

/**
 * Get the UNIT partno.
 * @return Value of partno.
 */
public String getPartno() {return partno;}

/**
 * Set the UNIT partno.
 * @param v  Value to assign to partno.
 */
public void setPartno(String  v) {this.partno = v;}

String serialno;

/**
 * Get UNIT serialno.
 * @return Value of serialno.
 */
public String getSerialno() {return serialno;}

/**
 * Set the UNIT serialno.
 * @param v  Value to assign to serialno.
 */
public void setSerialno(String  v) {this.serialno = v;}

float weight;

/**
 * Get the UNIT weight.
 * @return Value of weight.
 */
public float getWeight() {return weight;}
```

```
/**
 * Set the UNIT weight.
 * @param v  Value to assign to weight.
 */
/* public void setWeight(float  v) {this.weight = v;} */

public void setWeight(float f) throws BadWeightException {
    if (f <= 0.0) {
        BadWeightException b = new BadWeightException();
        throw b;
    }
    else {
        weight = f;
    }
}


int colorid;

/**
 * Get the UNIT colorid.
 * @return Value of colorid.
 */
public int getColorid() {return colorid;}

/**
 * Set the UNIT colorid.
 * @param v  Value to assign to colorid.
 */
public void setColorid(int  v) {this.colorid = v;}

int mfgid;

/**
 * Get the UNIT mfgid.
 * @return Value of mfgid.
 */
public int getMfgid() {return mfgid;}

/**
 * Set the UNIT mfgid.
 * @param v  Value to assign to mfgid.
 */
public void setMfgid(int  v) {this.mfgid = v;}

java.util.Date cdate;
```

```java
/**
   * Get the value of cdate.
   * @return Value of cdate.
   */
public java.util.Date getCdate() {return cdate;}

/**
   * Set the value of cdate.
   * @param v  Value to assign to cdate.
   */
public void setCdate(java.util.Date  v) {this.cdate = v;}


java.util.Date mdate;

/**
   * Get the value of mdate.
   * @return Value of mdate.
   */
public java.util.Date getMdate() {return mdate;}

/**
   * Set the value of mdate.
   * @param v  Value to assign to mdate.
   */
public void setMdate(java.util.Date  v) {this.mdate = v;}

String parentname;

/**
   * Get the value of parentname.
   * @return Value of parentname.
   */
public String getParentname() {return parentname;}

/**
   * Set the value of parentname.
   * @param v  Value to assign to parentname.
   */
public void setParentname(String  v) {this.parentname = v;}

/**
 * This is a method you can use to quickly view the object's contents.
 *  You may want to override this if you want to use this object
 *  in a GUI control or widget.
 *
 *  In this form, you can just do:
 *  System.out.println(unitinfo);
 *  ...and get a nice listing of the object values.
```

```
     *
     * @param nil a value of type ''
     * @return a value of type 'String'
     */
    public String toString() {
        String s = "id: " + getId() + "\n" +
            "name: " + getName() + "\n" +
            "parentid:" + getParentid() + "\n" +
            "partno: " + getPartno() + "\n" +
            "serialno: " + getSerialno() + "\n" +
            "weight: " + getWeight() + "\n" +
            "colorid: " + getColorid() + "\n" +
            "mfgid: " + getMfgid() + "\n" +
            "cdate: " + getCdate() + "\n" +
            "mdate: " + getMdate() + "\n" +
            "parentname: " + getParentname() + "\n";
        return s;
    }


} // UnitInfo
```

Chapter 3

The RMI Server

- ▼ QUICK START
- ▼ TECHNOLOGY OVERVIEW
- ▼ RMI UNDER 1.2 VS. 1.1
- ▼ HOW APPLICATIONS FIND REMOTE OBJECTS:
  THE RMI REGISTRY
- ▼ THE RMI OBJECT SERVERS
- ▼ SHELL SCRIPTS FOR YOUR SERVERS
- ▼ ORGANIZING YOUR SYSTEM
- ▼ SHARING FILES

Quick Start

In the last chapter we built a database API based on RMI. This chapter tells you how to set up your RMI server for your clients to access the database API. Examples of shell scripts for starting and stopping your server are given, as well as example file-system layouts.

Technology Overview

In our application, the RMI server will function as your broker, or middle tier, to the database. However, it gives you much more than that. Besides making your database API accessible remotely, it also helps you centralize any other logic or relocatable code modules, making your clients lighter and easier to manage. In addition, your developers will be able to make simple method calls to access the database rather than have to open sockets and other network programming tasks. This makes application development simpler and more accessible by a broader range of developers.

RMI builds a dynamic network protocol for you, that relieves you from the work of designing that protocol yourself and dealing with the network socket implementation. RMI connectivity is stateless (it does not maintain persistent connections between itself and the clients), and happens on random high port numbers managed by RMI all transparently to the developer.

All objects passed via RMI—either passed in to methods or returned from them—need to be streamed over the network. Therefore, they need to implement the java.io.Serializable interface. Most Java primitives and commonly used classes like String are serializable. Other classes that you create to encapsulate your data will have to implement this interface.

With the database API complete we can setup the RMI portion of the system. An RMI server can be setup very quickly, but there are some administration details that you need to be aware of.

RMI Under 1.2 vs. 1.1

JDK 1.2 has a more configurable and complex security model than 1.1 does. If you're using 1.2, you'll need to find your java.policy file usually located in $JAVA_HOME/jre/lib/security. This is a simple text file that enables a system administrator to control what Java is allowed to do on the system. In that file you'll need to enable Java to make socket connections on ports 80 and > 1024. To accomplish this you'll need to make an addition like this:

```
grant {
    permission java.net.SocketPermission "*:1024-65535",
        "connect,accept";
    permission java.net.SocketPermission "*:80", "connect";
};
```

Note that the * allows any host to connect. If you wish, you can choose to configure this so that only certain hosts can connect.

JDK 1.1 does not require a java.policy file and relies on security managers instead.

How Applications Find Remote Objects: The RMI Registry

Most of us these days are familiar with DNS, or at least have heard of it. DNS is a naming service that translates human-readable names to Internet Protocol (IP) addresses. For instance, *www.foobar.com* gets resolved by DNS as the IP address 10.10.10.15. Likewise, the JDK includes a class called the RMI Registry that functions for our remote objects just like a DNS server tracks the machines it knows about. The RMI Registry keeps a list of human-readable names representing each of your objects that you are making available.

For instance, let's say that you have three objects that you want to make available. The object names might be something like *com.mycompany.MyDatabaseImpl*, *com.anothercompany.FooBarImpl*, and *ElephantTalkImpl*. The registry gives you the opportunity to alias these class names to something easier for your developers to recognize. So you bind a string to the object in the registry. You decide to bind "DATABASE" to *com.mycompany.MyDatabaseImpl*. Now your clients can ask for "DATABASE" and get a handle to *com.mycompany.MyDatabaseImpl*. What names you bind to your objects is entirely up to you. However, it is something you will need to administer if you have many developers publishing objects.

You start up the registry first as an independent process. From a shell you could run something like this:

```
$ rmiregistry &
```

That will work of course, and you now have a server you could start registering objects to. However, in the real world, that will never do. If this is going to be part of a system that runs 24/7, then you can't have it rely on you starting it up out of your account on the server. What you really need is for this service to light itself up at boot in the same way a service like DNS or HTTP would.

This means you're going to have to write some shell scripts. What? I'm supposed to be writing in Java! Well, one thing not ordinarily covered in books on Java programming is that it's pretty impractical to type things like:

```
$JAVA_HOME/bin/java -classpath ./foo/bar:boinx.jar:. MyClass
```

at the command line. There's too much that could go wrong. Good shell scripts are critical to making sure that your classes get loaded with the proper environment, not to mention making sure your software works at all. How many times have you tried to run a demo of some new Java technology only to see it fail? Nine times out of ten, it's the fault of the shell script shipped with the software. It's unbelievable to watch all the time that went in to the development of something wasted by the poor execution of a simple shell script.

The best way to figure out how to write shell scripts is to look at one of the venerable scripts living in /etc/init.d. These are very well crafted Bourne shell scripts meant to be invoked on startup of a Unix server. A good method to get your own startup script going is to copy one of these scripts and hack it to your needs. Remember, you want to maintain the basic functionality and structure of the script, so that it will behave in a manner expected by both the server and your system administrator.

Here's a simple example shell script for starting up the RMI Registry.

```sh
#!/bin/sh
CLASSPATH=
PIDFILE="rmid.pid"

case $1 in
'start')
    java sun.rmi.registry.RegistryImpl &
    echo $! > $PIDFILE
    ;;
'stop')
    kill -9 `cat $PIDFILE`
    rm $PIDFILE
    ;;
*)
    echo "usage:rmid start/stop"
    ;;
esac
```

You can invoke this script from the command line by typing:

```
rmid start
```

And you stop it with:

```
rmid stop
```

Or you can place it with your other boot scripts and it will start up the server on boot for you.

The script writes some information to a log, and records its process ID to a file. This is analogous to the way many Web servers are configured. As such, the process shouldn't be too unfamiliar to your system administrators. This will make them happy, and you look good.

Notice that we've set the CLASSPATH to null. The reason for this is that if the value of CLASSPATH is not null, the registry will try to use the value of CLASS-PATH instead of the java.rmi.server.codebase property to locate your stub classes to transmit to the client. As you start up multiple object servers, you will start to run into all sorts of problems. This will be clearer when we actually start going over the server code. For now, just make sure your RMI Registry is always started with no CLASSPATH.

Also note that instead of using the RMI Registry script included with the JDK, we call the class directly. This is simply so that we can capture the process ID of the actual registry class instead of the calling script so that we can kill it when when we invoke the stop command. On some platforms, the provided RMI Registry tool is either a shell script or a C wrapper. In either case, it simply sets up the environment and then calls sun.rmi.registry.RegistryImpl.

The RMI Object Servers

First of all, the Java code for your database API object server:

Listing 3–1: UnitDBServer.java

```java
import java.util.*;
import java.rmi.*;
import java.rmi.registry.*;
import java.rmi.server.*;
/**
 * UnitDBServer.java
 *
 * A simple RMI Server wrapper that makes use of properties.
 * This class writes to STDOUT and STDERR, so that when
 * debugging you can monitor the status from the command line,
 * or redirect the output to log and error files as is common
 * with unix servers.
 *
 * Created: Mon Oct 11 22:32:52 1999
 *
 * @author Stewart Birnam
 * @version 1.0
 */

public class UnitDBServer {

    public UnitDBServer() {

    }

    public static void main(String[] args) {

        // load a security manager if one already isnt in place...
        if (System.getSecurityManager() == null) {
            System.setSecurityManager(new RMISecurityManager());
        }

        // check for properties
        Properties p = System.getProperties();
        String rminame = p.getProperty("unitdb.rminame");
        String dbuser = p.getProperty("unitdb.dbuser");
        String pass = p.getProperty("unitdb.pass");
        String hostname = p.getProperty("unitdb.hostname");
        String instance = p.getProperty("unitdb.instance");

        /*----------------------------------------------------------*
         *  one way or another, we spit out the properties we started
```

```
 *  with to stdout since our shell script redirects this to a
 *  log file, we can easily check how the server was invoked
 *  after the fact.
 *-------------------------------------------------------------------------*/

        p.save(System.out, "Starting UnitDb Server with the following properties");

        try {
            UnitDbImpl u;
            if (dbuser != null || pass != null ||
                hostname != null || instance != null) {
                u = new UnitDbImpl(dbuser, pass, hostname, instance);
            } else {
                // use defaults
                u = new UnitDbImpl();
            }

            if (rminame != null) {
                Naming.rebind(rminame, u);
            } else {
                Naming.rebind("UNITDB", u);
            }
        }
        catch (java.net.MalformedURLException me) {
            me.printStackTrace();
            System.exit(1);
        }
        catch (RemoteException re) {
            re.printStackTrace();
            System.exit(1);
        }
    }
}

} // UnitDBServer
```

There's a bit more code in here than you might usually see in a typical RMI server example. That's because we want to be able to have some flexibility in our design. Because it's a server piece, I want to be able to start it from the command line in the same way I might start another Unix service. One easy way to get parameters from the command line to your software is to make use of the System.getProperties() method. This enables us to pass in parameters to Java with the -D option. We can then set the actual parameters in our wrapper shell script, as follows:

Listing 3–2: unitdbd

```sh
#!/bin/sh

    ##-----------------------------------------------------------------------------
    ## configure the following options as needed
    ##-----------------------------------------------------------------------------

RMINAME="-Dunitdb.rminame=UNITDB"
DBUSER="-Dunitdb.dbuser=stewartb"
PASS="-Dunitdb.pass=stewartb"
HOSTNAME="-Dunitdb.hostname=localhost"
INSTANCE="-Dunitdb.instance=book"

    ##-----------------------------------------------------------------------------
    ##  the following may need to change based on your system configuration...
    ##-----------------------------------------------------------------------------

JAVA_HOME="/usr/java"
ORACLE_HOME="/usr/local/oracle"
CLASSPATH="$JAVA_HOME/lib/classes.zip:$ORACLE_HOME/jdbc/lib/classes111.zip:."
PIDFILE="unitdb.pid"
LOGFILE="unitdb.log"
ERRFILE="unitdb.err"

OPTIONS="$RMINAME $DBUSER $PASS $HOSTNAME $INSTANCE"

case $1 in
'start')
    java $OPTIONS -Djava.rmi.server.codebase=file:/home/stewartb/thebook/src/
    UnitDBServer\
        1> $LOGFILE 2> $ERRFILE &
    echo $! > $PIDFILE
    ;;
'stop')
    kill `cat $PIDFILE`
    rm $PIDFILE
    ;;
*)
    echo "usage: unitdbd start/stop"
    ;;
esac
```

This helps makes the software administration more familiar to sysadmins and
non-Java programmers.

Organizing Your System

You can lay out your system any way you wish (and most developers do), however I put forth the notion that if you follow some basic conventions used in the Unix file system, you can make your system more recognizable and easier to administer by others. I'm going to assume for the rest of this book that you are going to use the same machine as middle tier and file server. Here is an example directory structure you may want to follow:

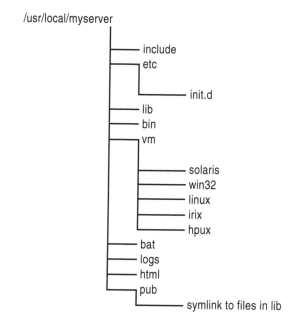

- Include: Here you can put any reusable shell script fragments or environment setups to make writing your shell scripts easier.

- Etc: Configuration files commonly go here. The subdirectory init.d is where you will put all your server startup/shutdown scripts.

- Lib: All your class files will go here, organized into whatever subdirectories are necessary for your packages. You can also configure your Web server to access servlets from this directory as well.

- Bin: All executable client shell scripts live here. These can be run over NFS if desired.

- Vm [OPTIONAL]: You can install fully configured JVMs in this directory grouped by OS. Your clients can mount the server and run the VM locally using your install from a remote (NFS or Samba) drive. While loading the files over the Net may take a few seconds longer than running it off a local disk, the savings in individual workstation installation and configuration are huge. If you're running a 100baseT Ethernet LAN this shouldn't be much of an issue for you anyway. With this system, you can manage everyone's Java installation from a single machine. This will greatly minimize problems you may encounter with users installing different VMs or accidentally deleting them to free up disk space. This is worth trying as it has the potential to save you significant pain and frustration.

- Bat: You'll put the MS-DOS batch file versions of the shell scripts you put in bin here and serve them up via Samba.

- Logs: Log files for each of the servers you setup, as well as the RMI Registry.

- Html: All that documentation you've been writing can go here. You may also be deploying servlets and need a place to put your ancillary HTML files. It may be advantageous to mirror some of the JVM software here if you do have to deploy to each machine.

- Pub: The anonymous FTP site. Symlinks to your classes, or to the JVM installations you're mirroring can be found here. In the event your clients can't use NFS or Samba, you can at least have a central repository to distribute from.

Sharing Files

You'll need to make sure your server is setup to make the directories you want available to your users via NFS, HTTP, FTP, and Samba. You should consult with your system administrator to make sure not only that the services are running, but that you are granting read-only access to your files. Depending on how secure your environment is and your application needs, you may want to restrict access based on group permissions or some other method. It's not required to implement all these protocols, your system may only require one—if any at all. However, they are not very hard to set up and very useful to have.

Check out Chapter 7 for more information on software distribution via NFS, Samba, and HTTP/FTP.

Chapter 4

The Swing Client

Quick Start

Now that we finally have our servers and database API in place, we can start concentrating on our GUI clients. To build our GUI, we're going to use the rich feature set available with Swing, sometimes referred to as the Java foundation classes.

Programming examples of dialogs are given, using RMI and Jtree with data from the Database API. Some discussion of threading in Swing and JTable is provided.

Technology Overview

The JFC (Java foundation classes)—otherwise known as Swing—is part of the Java 2 core API and available for use with Java 1.1 as a separate package. The JFC is a very feature-rich set of classes to be used in GUI client development. Unlike the original AWT, or other graphical toolkits available, the JFC provides many high-level widgets that address the needs of modern application development. Tables or grids, trees, ComboBoxes, ScrollPanes, and StyledText objects are all in residence. Even the primitive GUI objects like buttons and text fields have a complete set of usable methods available. In addition, many of these objects have specialized data models and listeners provided. The result is a vast savings in application development time and the power to implement complex user-required features without custom widget creation.

Look and Feel

The Look and Feel (L&F) implementation is an additional advantage to using the JFC. This enables you to change the "look and feel" of your application as it migrates from Windows to MacOS to Unix without any additional coding. Better still, rather than your application morphing as it moves between platforms, you can simply use the default L&F called Metal. Using the Metal L&F has two main advantages. First of all, professional designers built it, so it looks good without any additional noodling by the developer. Second, it provides a uniform L&F cross-platform.

While it's great that your application can appear "Windows-ish" or "Mac-like" or "Motif-ized" on Windows, Macintosh, and Unix, this flexibility should be examined from a documentation standpoint. Using a cross-platform L&F means you only need one screen snapshot instead of one for each operating system. It will also make it easier for your support staff when answering questions about the application to have a unified L&F to the application. In short, save yourself a lot of hassle and use the default L&F. It looks great, and it's just plain easier.

Lightweight vs. Heavyweight and Cutting and Pasting

The original AWT made use of *native peers* for all its GUI components. That is, for every java.awt.Button object created, another object was created using the native operating system's GUI libraries. Swing builds all its components using Java without native peers. This makes the application use fewer system resources to do the same amount of work. The drawback is that having native peers in all your text fields meant that you could use cut and paste between applications, even though Java itself didn't support it.

However, you can mix heavyweight and lightweight components if you need to with some trickery. The important thing to remember is that the Z-order of the heavyweight objects will be in front of the lightweight objects. Also, if you're placing heavyweight objects inside of lightweight containers, you'll need to make sure that the heavyweight object's preferredSize is set, otherwise the light-weight container might not know how to display it properly.

JFC As a Separate Package

One drawback with the JFC—particularly if you're using it with Java 1.1—is that you'll have to tote around the roughly 1.2 MB swingall.jar file. (Later I'll show you some distribution strategies to help you avoid painful installation.) However, this file is worth its weight. You won't find a more feature-laden set of GUI widgets anywhere, particularly for free. And if you've ever tried to build GUI applications using beasts like Tk or Motif or even the original AWT, you'll be overjoyed at the power and flexibility that Swing provides. Furthermore, it is arguable that in today's 12 Gigs for $250 marketplace that 1.2 Megs is nothing anyway.

The Swing API is gigantic. It will take you some time to master it, and dig through all its nooks and crannies. However the time investment is well worth it. You'll find in the long run that you'll be able to build powerful, feature-rich GUIs quickly and easily, even without using a visual builder (not that I've seen any visual builders that really work well).

For more information on the internals of Swing, or a more in-depth tour of the APIs, consult the online documentation at *java.sun.com/jfc* or check out one of the many fine books on Swing. For purposes of our example, we'll just dive in and start using Swing to illustrate some common application development techniques.

Programming Concepts

Preparing for the Worst—Handling Your Exceptions and Displaying Dialogs

Things will always break, and no matter how smart you are, you're going to make mistakes. One simple way to display your mistakes proudly to the world is to use the JOptionPane class. For instance, in this GUI, I have included the following method:

```
public void displayError(Exception e) {
  JOptionPane.showMessageDialog(null, e);
  System.exit(1);
}
```

This makes use of one of the many static methods of the JOptionPane class. It presents a simple modal alert dialog, with the message from the exception displayed in it. See Figure 4–1.

Figure 4–1: JOptionPane displaying an error

You can also add additional information by creating your own exception with your desired message, and then adding the original error message if you wish.

```
catch (RemoteException re) {
    Exception e = new Exception("Cannot connect to database.\n" +
                                re.getMessage());
    displayError(e);
}
```

Starting RMI from a GUI

There is nothing you need to do any different in terms of getting a handle to a remote object from a GUI. Like in a command-line client, you may want to seed the instantiation of the remote object from information entered by the user. The only difference being that you will now get the data from a GUI component rather than from STDIN, and you'll need to display a modal dialog box in the event of some kind of failure creating the remote object. In our case, we'll use the displayError() method we've already created.

```
public void initRMI(String host, String rname) {
    try {
        String url = "rmi://" + host + "/";
        unitdb = (UnitDb) Naming.lookup(url + rname);
    }
    catch (Exception e) {
        displayError(e);
    }
}
```

Placing the initialization of the RMI object in a separate method gives us great flexibility. First of all, we can create the object from various constructors.

Assuming a default host and object name for the application:

```
public UnitDbClient() {
    initRMI("myhost", "myobject");
}
```

Allowing the host and object name to be specified at runtime:

```
public UnitDbClient(String n, String h) {
    RMINAME = n;
    RMIHOST = h;
    initRMI(h, n);
}
```

Allowing the object to be passed in by reference:

```
public UnitDbClient(UnitDb u) {
    unitdb = u;
}
```

Passing the remote object in by reference enables you to embed your application as a panel of another application. If the parent application already has a handle on the remote object, you can simply make use of the existing object rather than instantiating your own.

Another feature is you can reconnect to the object if necessary at runtime. By examining the exceptions you're trapping, you can determine if you need to reinitalize the object. This would be necessary if the database went down, failed over, or if the object server needed to be restarted.

Threading with Swing

Every book or Web page I've read on this subject suggests you should avoid threading in Swing. My experience confirms this. The reason is not that it won't work for you; if you use the correct methods recommended by the Swing designers, it works perfectly. The real reason is you set up your application for increased complexity, and create the potential for deadlocks. It just makes your code more difficult to maintain and debug. And changes in components of the distributed system may have an adverse effect on the behavior of your application.

Here's an example: Let's say you decide to thread an operation that takes a long time to retrieve data from a slow remote server. This is an excellent reason to consider using a thread, and by doing so you make the GUI responsive while it waits for the data. This enhances *perceived* performance. Because the GUI doesn't block on the remote call, it *looks* like it's going faster, even though it's not.

Finally, someone decides to fix the real problem by replacing the slow server with a fast one. Suddenly, your application can receive its data four times faster. You may inadvertently find yourself in some kind of deadlock situation due to other operations not being able to complete in the way they used to while the other thread was waiting for remote data. In the end it's not worth all the trouble you went to, and you end up ripping all the threading out as it's no longer necessary anyway.

You also must consider why does the GUI need to be responsive while the user waits for database access? Do you really want the user entering more data while you're in the middle of a transaction? Probably not. Unless you want to throw up a progress bar or animated hourglass, stay away from threads.

If you must forge ahead with threads, the packages you'll need to examine are SwingUtilities, SwingWorker, and Timer.

There are excellent tutorials on threads in Swing available at Sun's Swing Connection, at *java.sun.com/jfc*.

Populating Your Widgets with Data from Remote Objects

Typically in database applications you need to keep track of not only what the user sees in the GUI, but also maintain an association between that data and a primary key. One example is a picklist table that contains two columns, a sequence number, and a text description. In our database, we have a table called COLOR. It looks like this:

```
CREATE TABLE COLOR (
    ID      NUMBER constraint pk_color primary key,
    NAME    VARCHAR2(20)
)
```

One way to solve this problem is to make use of the java.util.Hashtable class. This class maintains a table of key—value pairs. Both the keys and the values can be extracted as enumerations. Both keys and values are objects, so you can map more than just a string to a number if you wish.

The Model-View Architecture

ComboBoxes. A common task for a database programmer is to provide a popup list of items retrieved from the database. For our example, we want the person doing data entry to enter a color for each product. We want to force the user to enter only the approved colors in the database. To achieve this, we'll use the Swing JComboBox class. I like this class for several reasons. One, it provides a scrolling popup menu, so you don't have to worry about long menus rolling off the screen or building hierarchical menus. Two, the selected value remains displayed so the user can remember what they've chosen without invoking the menu again. Finally, you can make the textfield that displays the value editable, so that you could have the user enter more items into the list if you wanted.

One of the easiest ways to deal with picklists is with the hashtable class we discussed earlier. We can use the Hashtable.keys() method to pull out the list needed for the JComboBox. We already have a method in the UnitDb Interface that gives us what we need:

```
public Hashtable getColor() throws RemoteException;
```

and the corresponding method to our implementation:

```
public Hashtable getColor() throws RemoteException {
        Hashtable h = new Hashtable();
        String sql = "select id, name from color";
        try {
            Statement stmt = conn.createStatement();
            ResultSet rs = stmt.executeQuery(sql);
            if ( rs.next() == false ) {
                rs.close();
                stmt.close();
```

```
                } else {
                  do {
                      h.put(rs.getString(2), new Integer(rs.getInt(1)));
                  }
                  while (rs.next()) ;

                    rs.close();
                    stmt.close();
                }
            }
            catch (SQLException e) {
                RemoteException re = new
                    RemoteException(e.getMessage());
                throw re;
            }
            return h;
    }
```

The implementation builds us a java.util.Hashtable object that contains the color name (string) as the key, and the color ID (integer) as the value. This is not as you might expect it to be organized, being exactly the opposite from the way it's stored in the database. However, it will all become clear when we try to apply this data structure to our GUI widget.

First, we acquire the hashtable by referencing the method from our handle on the remote object:

```
try {
    colorhash = unitdb.getColor();
}
catch (RemoteException re) {
    Exception e = new Exception("Cannot connect to database.\n" +
                                    re.getMessage());
    displayError(e);
}
catch (Exception ee) {
    displayError(ee);
}
```

Later, we seed the JComboBox with the keys from the hashtable:

```
Vector v = new Vector();
for (Enumeration e = colorhash.keys() ; e.hasMoreElements() ;) {
    v.addElement(e.nextElement());
}

DefaultComboBoxModel colormodel = new DefaultComboBoxModel(v);
JComboBox colorcombo = new JComboBox(colormodel);
```

A few lines of code, but a lot of data flying around. Here's what we're doing: First, we create a vector for temporary storage and to seed the DefaultComboBoxModel later on. Next, we yank all the keys out of the hashtable with the keys() method call. This returns an enumeration, which we iterate through in order to build up the contents of the vector. That being done, we then seed a DefaultComboBoxModel object with the vector. (We use the DefaultComboBoxModel object for the method calls it provides, which will be of use over the life of the application.)

This gives us a popup menu that looks like Figure 4–2.

So, the user is presented with the list of colors. When the user selects a color, you can then translate that into the information you need to interact with the database, namely the primary key or id for that color. You query the widget with a call like this:

```
Integer I = (Integer) colorhash.get(colorcombo.getSelectedItem());
```

getSelectedItem() returns the object currently selected by the user. We then pass that into our hash to retrieve the database key for that color.

That seems so convoluted. Can't I just use the colors themselves as keys?

You could. The problem stems from the fact that the color names are determined by humans. As such, you can guarantee that after some period of time, "Yellow" will be changed to "Sunshine" or "Yellow Submarine". If that update occurs while your application is running, then any queries about "Yellow" would become void, versus queries regarding key 23 would still be valid.

Furthermore, you can query the UNIT table without joining back to the COLOR table if you already have the key. The fewer joins you make, the more efficient the query will be. Remember, every time you ask the database a question, it's potentially expensive. Doing whatever you can to cache data and make your database calls more efficient will increase performance and promote scalability.

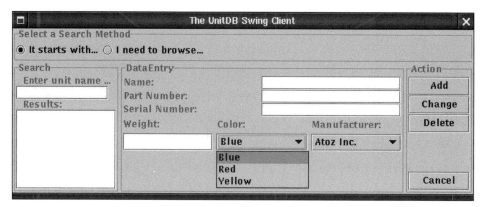

Figure 4–2: JComboBox in action

JTree database browser. You can easily build a tree view of a hierarchical database relationship. The important concept here is that the JTree API lets you attach your own user-defined object to each node in the tree. These objects correspond to the records in your database. They can contain as much or as little information as you want. However, they will need to contain enough information for you to identify them back to the database.

For our tree, we will create an object called UnitNode, as follows:

Listing 4–1: UnitNode.java

```
public class UnitNode implements Serializable {

    public UnitNode() {

    }

    public UnitNode (int i, int j, String s) {
        id = i;
        parentid = j;
        name = s;
    }

    int id;
    public int getId() {return id;}
    public void setId(int   v) {this.id = v;}

    int parentid;
    public int getParentid() {return parentid;}
    public void setParentid(int   v) {this.parentid = v;}

    String name;
    public String getName() {return name;}
    public void setName(String   v) {this.name = v;}

    String parentname;
    public String getParentname() {return parentname;}
    public void setParentname(String   v) {this.parentname = v;}

    public String toString() {
        return name;
    }
}
```

Since you have the potential to pull every record from your database down via some enthusiastic tree browsing, you probably don't want to have the entire contents of each record come across for every leaf in the tree. Better that you define just what you need; in this case, the name of the unit, the name of the parent unit, and the keys for both.

Now, to actually build the tree. We want our class to extend JPanel so that we can place the tree inside of any container we wish. We add to the panel a JScrollPane that contains our JTree. This will enable scrolling as the tree dynamically grows. We also add a default listener, so that the tree will work right out of the box. However, we'll also put in a method so that the developer can add her own custom listener to the tree.

Listing 4–2: UnitTreeBrowser.java

```java
import java.io.*;
import java.rmi.*;
import java.util.*;
import java.awt.*;
import java.awt.event.*;

import javax.swing.*;
import javax.swing.tree.*;
import javax.swing.event.*;

/**
 * UnitTreeBrowser.java
 *
 *
 * Created: Wed Nov  3 20:31:33 1999
 *
   @author (c) 1999, 2000 Stewart Birnam
 * @version  1.0
 */

public class UnitTreeBrowser extends JPanel {
    UnitDb unitdb;
    /*----------------------------------------------------------------------*
     *   Data Structure Globals
     *----------------------------------------------------------------------*/
    UnitNode TOP_NODE = new UnitNode(0,0,"UnitDB");
    UnitNode LAST_NODE = new UnitNode(0,0,"temp");
    public DefaultMutableTreeNode TOP_TREE = new DefaultMutableTreeNode(TOP_NODE);
    /*----------------------------------------------------------------------*
     *   GUI Globals
     *----------------------------------------------------------------------*/
    public JTree tree;
    TreeSelectionListener TSL;
    JScrollPane treeview;

    public UnitTreeBrowser(UnitDb u) {
       // get our handle on the database object
       unitdb = u;
       // seed the tree with a default "root" object
       tree = new JTree(TOP_TREE);
       // force single selection mode on our tree
       tree.getSelectionModel().setSelectionMode(
                          TreeSelectionModel.SINGLE_TREE_SELECTION);
```

```java
        // place out tree in a scrolling pane.
        treeview = new JScrollPane(tree);

        createNodes(TOP_TREE); // grab some initial data from the database
        TSL = new DefaultUnitTreeListener(); // add our default listener

        tree.addTreeSelectionListener(TSL);
        setLayout(new BorderLayout());
        add(treeview, "Center");
    }

/** This method allows the developer to add their own listener to the tree */
    public void addTreeListener(TreeSelectionListener t) {
        tree.removeTreeSelectionListener(TSL);
        TSL = t;
        tree.addTreeSelectionListener(TSL);
    }

    /* add leaves on the tree based on whatever falls below
    /* the passed in DefaultMutableTreeNode */
    public void createNodes(DefaultMutableTreeNode top) {
        DefaultMutableTreeNode unit = null;
        Vector v;
        try {
            UnitNode u = (UnitNode) top.getUserObject();
            v = unitdb.getChildUnits(u.getId());
            for (int i=0; i < v.size(); i++) {
                UnitNode p = (UnitNode) v.elementAt(i);
                unit = new DefaultMutableTreeNode(p);

                top.add(unit);
            }
        }
        catch (RemoteException re) {
            re.printStackTrace();
        }

    }

    public class DefaultUnitTreeListener implements TreeSelectionListener {
        public void valueChanged(TreeSelectionEvent e) {
            DefaultMutableTreeNode node = (DefaultMutableTreeNode)
              (e.getPath().getLastPathComponent());

            Object node_object = node.getUserObject();
            UnitNode unitnode = (UnitNode)node_object;

            if (node.isLeaf()) {
                createNodes(node);
            }

        }
    }
}
```

```
        /* a main method is added to test the object as a standalone panel */
        public static void main(String[] args) {

            String RMIHOST = "kehleyr";
            String RMINAME = "UNITDB";

            UnitDb unitdb;
            UnitTreeBrowser p;

            JFrame frame = new JFrame("TreeBrowser");
            WindowListener l = new WindowAdapter() {
                public void windowClosing(WindowEvent e) {System.exit(0);}
            };

            try {
                String url = "rmi://" + RMIHOST + "/";
                unitdb = (UnitDb) Naming.lookup(url + RMINAME);
                p = new UnitTreeBrowser(unitdb);
                System.out.println("Connected to database");
                frame.getContentPane().add(p);

            }
            catch (Exception e) {e.printStackTrace();}

            frame.addWindowListener(l);
            frame.setSize(400,400);

            frame.pack();
            frame.show();
        }

} // UnitTreeBrowser
```

A couple of things to note: This class does not instantiate its own copy of the UnitDb class. Rather a reference to an existing one is passed in to the tree in its constructor. Second, this class has a main method. The main method is only invoked when the object is invoked directly from the command line. As in:

```
java    UnitTreeBrowser
```

If the class is instantiated from another class, as in:

```
UnitTreeBrowser tree = new UnitTreeBrowser(untidb);
```

then the main method will not be called. The purpose of the main method is solely to be able to test the object on its own without having to debug it inside of another application.

TIP: Give all your objects a main method. It will keep you safe, while demonstrating the usage of the object to other developers.

Once you have your object created and stored in the tree, you use a listener that
you define to read the contents out of the node-defined object and take whatever
action is appropriate. For instance, the default listener included does this:

```
public class DefaultUnitTreeListener implements TreeSelectionListener {

    // the TreeSelectionLIstener interface only requires
    // us to implement valueChanged().
    public void valueChanged(TreeSelectionEvent e) {
        // first we get a handle on the tree node selected
        DefaultMutableTreeNode node = (DefaultMutableTreeNode)
        (e.getPath().getLastPathComponent());
        // then we pull our user defined object out of the node.
        Object node_object = node.getUserObject();
        // cast it back into our UnitNode object
        UnitNode unitnode = (UnitNode)node_object;
        // test to see if the selected node is a leaf.
        // If it is, populate the branch.
        if (node.isLeaf()) {
            createNodes(node);
        }
    }
}
```

The default listener provides you with some expected behavior, although typically you would override it, as we do in our client.

```
public class UnitTreeListener implements TreeSelectionListener {
    public void valueChanged(TreeSelectionEvent e) {
        current_node = (DefaultMutableTreeNode)
        (e.getPath().getLastPathComponent());

        Object node_object = current_node.getUserObject();
        UnitNode unitnode = (UnitNode)node_object;

        if (current_node.isLeaf()) {
            treepanel.createNodes(current_node);
        }
        // our addition. Populate the rest of the GUI by
        // querying the database for the record indicated
        // by the tree selection
        try {
            setUnitInfo(unitdb.getUnitInfo(unitnode.getId()));
        }
        catch (RemoteException re) {
            displayError(re);
        }

    }
}
```

The setUnitInfo method above actually populates the widgets in the GUI with values extracted from the UnitInfo object. You could include other methods that fired off other behaviors based on what the user selected in the tree. The point is, you have to insert some logic of your own into the listener or you just have a browsing tree.

Putting It All Together—The Actual Client

Ok, we have a stateless connection to the database via RMI, we have a system for handling popup lists, and we have classes for implementing a database-driven dynamic tree widget. Now it's time to make it sing and dance. When it's all done, it looks like Figures 4–3 through 4–6.

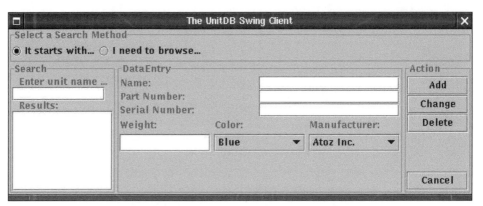

Figure 4–3: The UnitDbClient as it appears at startup

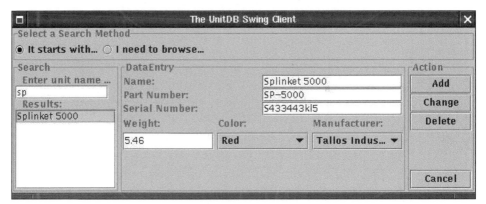

Figure 4–4: Entering a search string and choosing the result from the list, causing the fields to fill in

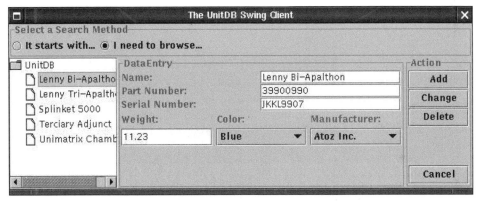

Figure 4–5: Activating the tree browser

Figure 4–6: Autopopulating the fields by selecting leaves on the tree

Here's the entire source code listing for the client, with a few comments along the way:

Listing 4–3: UnitDbClient.java

```
import javax.swing.*;
import java.awt.*;
import java.awt.event.*;
import java.util.*;
import java.rmi.*;
import java.io.*;
import javax.swing.tree.*;
import javax.swing.event.*;

/**
```

```
 * UnitDbClient.java
 *
 *
 * Created: Mon Oct 11 23:39:01 1999
 *
 * @author Stewart Birnam
 * @version 1.0
 */

public class UnitDbClient extends JPanel {

    /*-------------------------------------------------------------------------*
     *   GLOBALS
     *-------------------------------------------------------------------------*/

    String RMINAME = "UNITDB";
    String RMIHOST = "localhost";
    UnitDb unitdb;
    UnitInfo current_unit = new UnitInfo();
        // the object currently displayed in the gui


    /*-------------------------------------------------------------------------*
     *   GLOBAL WIDGETS
     *-------------------------------------------------------------------------*/
    JPanel cardpanel;
    JComboBox colorcombo, mfgcombo;
    JTextField namefield, partnofield, serialnofield, weightfield, queryfield;
    UnitTreeBrowser treepanel;
    DefaultMutableTreeNode current_node;
    JList resultlist;

    /*-------------------------------------------------------------------------*
     *   GLOBAL Data Structures for widgets
     *-------------------------------------------------------------------------*/

    Hashtable colorhash, mfghash, coloridhash, mfgidhash, queryhash;
    DefaultComboBoxModel colormodel, mfgmodel;
    DefaultListModel querylist;

    /**
     * Default Constructor. Uses hardcoded values.
     *
     */
    public UnitDbClient() {
        init();
    }
```

```java
/**
 * This constructor lets you specify the RMI object name in the registry as well
 * as the hostname.
 *
 * @param RMINAME, the name of the remote object in the registry -  a value of
 * type 'String' param HOSTNAME, the hostname of the RMI server - a value of
 * type @'String'
 */
public UnitDbClient(String n, String h) {
    RMINAME = n;
    RMIHOST = h;
    init();
}


/**
 * This constructor lets you pass in the remote object by reference.
 *
 * @param u a value of type 'UnitDb'
 */
public UnitDbClient(UnitDb u) {
    unitdb = u;
    init();
}


/*--------------------------------------------------------------------------*
 *  main Initialization setup - individual panel setups are called from here.
 *--------------------------------------------------------------------------*/

public void init() {
    // setup the RMI object if we don't already have it
    if (unitdb == null) {
        initRMI(RMIHOST, RMINAME);
    }

//populate our color and mfg hashes right away
    try {
        mfghash = unitdb.getMfg();
        colorhash = unitdb.getColor();
        // build reverse-lookup hashtables locally
        // you could make another call to the database, but
        // doing it on the client can boost performance significantly if
        // your database or net connection is slow
        Object elem = new Object();
        mfgidhash = new Hashtable();
        coloridhash = new Hashtable();
        for (Enumeration e = mfghash.keys() ; e.hasMoreElements() ;) {
            elem = e.nextElement();
            mfgidhash.put(mfghash.get(elem), elem);
        }
```

```
        for (Enumeration e = colorhash.keys() ; e.hasMoreElements() ;) {
            elem = e.nextElement();
            coloridhash.put(colorhash.get(elem), elem);
        }
    }
    catch (RemoteException re) {
        Exception e = new Exception("Cannot connect to database.\n" +
                                re.getMessage());
        displayError(e);
    }
    catch (Exception ee) {
        displayError(ee);
    }

    setLayout(new BorderLayout());

    JPanel toppanel = new JPanel();
    initSearchOptionPanel(toppanel);

    JPanel fieldpanel = new JPanel();
    initfieldpanel( fieldpanel );


    IUDPanel iudpanel = new IUDPanel(BoxLayout.Y_AXIS);
    iudpanel.setBorder(BorderFactory.createLoweredBevelBorder());
    IUDListener iudlistener = new IUDListener();
    iudpanel.insertbutton.addActionListener(iudlistener);
    iudpanel.updatebutton.addActionListener(iudlistener);
    iudpanel.deletebutton.addActionListener(iudlistener);
    iudpanel.cancelbutton.addActionListener(iudlistener);

    treepanel = new UnitTreeBrowser(unitdb);
    treepanel.addTreeListener(new UnitTreeListener());

    // expand the root node of the tree
    treepanel.tree.expandPath(treepanel.tree.getPathForRow(0));

    JPanel querypanel = new JPanel();
    initQueryPanel(querypanel);

    cardpanel = new JPanel();
    cardpanel.setLayout(new CardLayout());
    cardpanel.setPreferredSize(new Dimension(150,150));
        //keeps the inital size small
    cardpanel.add("RESULTPANEL", querypanel);
    cardpanel.add("TREEPANEL", treepanel);
```

```
        add(toppanel, "North");
        add(fieldpanel, "Center");
        add(iudpanel, "East");
        add(cardpanel, "West");

}


/*--------------------------------------------------------------------*
 * RMI initialization
 *-------------------------------------------------------------------*/


public void initRMI(String host, String rname) {
    try {
        String url = "rmi://" + host + "/";
        unitdb = (UnitDb) Naming.lookup(url + rname);
    }
    catch (Exception e) {
        displayError(e);
    }
}


/*--------------------------------------------------------------------*
 *   QUERY panel initialization
 *-------------------------------------------------------------------*/


void initQueryPanel(JPanel p) {

    p.setLayout(new BoxLayout(p, BoxLayout.Y_AXIS));
    p.setBorder(BorderFactory.createLoweredBevelBorder());


    JLabel label = new JLabel("Enter unit name here:");
    queryfield = new JTextField(10);
    //queryfield.setMaximumSize(queryfield.getPreferredSize());
    queryfield.addKeyListener(new QueryListener());

    JLabel resultlabel = new JLabel("Results:");


    querylist = new DefaultListModel();
    resultlist = new JList(querylist);
    resultlist.addListSelectionListener(new ResultListener());

    JScrollPane resultscroll = new JScrollPane(resultlist);
```

```java
        p.add(label);
        p.add(queryfield);
        p.add(resultlabel);
        p.add(Box.createRigidArea(new Dimension(5,0)));
        p.add(resultscroll);
        p.add(Box.createVerticalGlue());
    }

    /*------------------------------------------------------------------*
     * SEARCH OPTION panel init
     *------------------------------------------------------------------*/

    void initSearchOptionPanel(JPanel p) {
        JRadioButton startswithbutton, browsebutton;
        RadioListener radiolistener = new RadioListener();

        p.setBorder(BorderFactory.createTitledBorder("Search"));

        startswithbutton = new JRadioButton("It starts with...");
        startswithbutton.setActionCommand("STARTSWITH");
        startswithbutton.setSelected(true);
        startswithbutton.addActionListener(radiolistener);

        browsebutton = new JRadioButton("I need to browse...");
        browsebutton.setActionCommand("BROWSE");
        browsebutton.addActionListener(radiolistener);

        ButtonGroup choosegroup = new ButtonGroup();
        choosegroup.add(startswithbutton);
        choosegroup.add(browsebutton);

        p.setLayout(new BoxLayout(p, BoxLayout.X_AXIS));
        p.add(startswithbutton);
        p.add(browsebutton);

    }

    /*------------------------------------------------------------------*
     *   INIT the FieldPanel (center panel)
     *------------------------------------------------------------------*/

    void initfieldpanel(JPanel p) {

        p.setBorder(BorderFactory.createTitledBorder("DataEntry"));
        p.setLayout(new BoxLayout(p, BoxLayout.Y_AXIS));

        JPanel fieldgrid = new JPanel(new GridLayout(3,2));
```

```
    JLabel l = new JLabel("Name:");
    fieldgrid.add(l);

    namefield = new JTextField(30);
    namefield.setMaximumSize( namefield.getPreferredSize() );

    fieldgrid.add(namefield);

    l = new JLabel("Part Number:");
    fieldgrid.add(l);

    partnofield = new JTextField(30);
    partnofield.setMaximumSize( partnofield.getPreferredSize() );
    fieldgrid.add(partnofield);

    l = new JLabel("Serial Number:");
    fieldgrid.add(l);

    serialnofield = new JTextField(30);
    serialnofield.setMaximumSize( serialnofield.getPreferredSize() );

    fieldgrid.add(serialnofield);

    p.add(fieldgrid);

/*------------------------------------------------------------------*
 *  here we build another panel to cluster some widgets together
 *  in order to save space.
 *------------------------------------------------------------------*/

    JPanel clusterpanel = new JPanel();
    GridLayout grid = new GridLayout(2,3);
    clusterpanel.setLayout(grid);
    grid.setHgap(5);

    l = new JLabel("Weight:");
    clusterpanel.add(l);

    l = new JLabel("Color:");
    clusterpanel.add(l);

    l = new JLabel("Manufacturer:");
    clusterpanel.add(l);

    weightfield = new JTextField(10);
    clusterpanel.add(weightfield);
```

```
        Vector v = new Vector();
        for (Enumeration e = colorhash.keys() ; e.hasMoreElements() ;) {
            v.addElement(e.nextElement());
        }

        QSort qsort = new QSort(v);
        v = qsort.getSortedVector();

        colormodel = new DefaultComboBoxModel(v);
        colorcombo = new JComboBox(colormodel);
        clusterpanel.add(colorcombo);

        v = new Vector();
        for (Enumeration e = mfghash.keys() ; e.hasMoreElements() ;) {
            v.addElement(e.nextElement());
        }
        qsort.setVector(v);
        v = qsort.getSortedVector();

        mfgmodel = new DefaultComboBoxModel(v );
        mfgcombo = new JComboBox(mfgmodel);
        clusterpanel.add(mfgcombo);

        p.add(clusterpanel);
        clusterpanel.setMaximumSize(clusterpanel.getPreferredSize());
        p.add(Box.createVerticalGlue());
    }




    /*------------------------------------------------------------------*
     *   LISTENERS
     *
     *------------------------------------------------------------------*/




    /*------------------------------------------------------------------*
     *   the listener for the Insert-Update-Delete panel
     *------------------------------------------------------------------*/


public class IUDListener implements ActionListener {
    public void actionPerformed (ActionEvent e) {
        try {
            JButton b = (JButton) e.getSource();
            if (b.getActionCommand().equals("INSERT")) {
                UnitInfo u = getUnitInfo();
                if (current_unit != null) {
                    u.setParentid(current_unit.getId());
                }
                int id = unitdb.insertUnit(u);
```

```
            u.setId(id);
            current_unit = u;
            // make sure the tree is in use first
            if (current_node != null) {
              UnitNode unitnode = new UnitNode(id,
                        current_unit.getParentid(), current_unit.getName());
              DefaultTreeModel treemodel =
                (DefaultTreeModel) treepanel.tree.getModel() ;
              treemodel.insertNodeInto(new DefaultMutableTreeNode(unitnode),
                        current_node,  0);
            }
        }

        if (b.getActionCommand().equals("UPDATE")) {
            UnitInfo u = getUnitInfo();
            unitdb.updateUnit(u);
        }

        if (b.getActionCommand().equals("DELETE")) {
            int id = current_unit.getId();
            unitdb.deleteUnit(id);

            DefaultTreeModel treemodel = (DefaultTreeModel)
                        treepanel.tree.getModel();
            treemodel.removeNodeFromParent(current_node);

        }

    }
    catch (RemoteException re) {
        displayError(re);
    }
  }
}


/*-----------------------------------------------------------*
 *  A listener for the treebrowser
 *-----------------------------------------------------------*/

public class UnitTreeListener implements TreeSelectionListener {
    public void valueChanged(TreeSelectionEvent e) {
        current_node = (DefaultMutableTreeNode)
            (e.getPath().getLastPathComponent());

        Object node_object = current_node.getUserObject();
        UnitNode unitnode = (UnitNode)node_object;
```

```
            if (current_node.isLeaf()) {
                treepanel.createNodes(current_node);
            }

            try {
                setUnitInfo(unitdb.getUnitInfo(unitnode.getId()));
            }
            catch (RemoteException re) {
                displayError(re);
            }


        }
    }


/*----------------------------------------------------------------*
 *  a listener for the radio button chooser
 *----------------------------------------------------------------*/
class RadioListener implements ActionListener {

    public void actionPerformed(ActionEvent e) {

        CardLayout cl = (CardLayout)(cardpanel.getLayout());

        if (e.getActionCommand().equals("EXACT")) {
            cl.show(cardpanel, "RESULTPANEL");
        }

        if (e.getActionCommand().equals("STARTSWITH")) {
            cl.show(cardpanel, "RESULTPANEL");
        }

        if (e.getActionCommand().equals("BROWSE")) {
            cl.show(cardpanel, "TREEPANEL");
        }



    }
}


/*----------------------------------------------------------------*
 *  a listener for the query field
 *----------------------------------------------------------------*/
class QueryListener extends KeyAdapter {

    public void keyPressed(KeyEvent e) {
        if (e.getKeyCode() == KeyEvent.VK_ENTER) {
```

```
            try {
                queryhash = unitdb.findUnit(queryfield.getText());
                querylist.clear();
                for (Enumeration en = queryhash.keys();
                    en.hasMoreElements() ;) {
                    querylist.addElement(en.nextElement());
                }
            }
            catch (RemoteException re) {
                displayError(re);
            }
        }

    }

}


/*------------------------------------------------------------------*
 *  a listener for the Query Result JList
 *------------------------------------------------------------------*/
class ResultListener implements ListSelectionListener {
    public void valueChanged(ListSelectionEvent e) {
        Integer I = (Integer)
            queryhash.get(resultlist.getSelectedValue());
        try {
            setUnitInfo(unitdb.getUnitInfo(I.intValue()));
        }
        catch (RemoteException re) {
            displayError(re);
        }
    }
}


/*------------------------------------------------------------------*
 *  DB Code
 *------------------------------------------------------------------*/


/**
 * getUnitInfo returns a UnitInfo object for passing to the
 * UnitDb insert, and update methods. It builds the UnitInfo
 * object by pulling values from the current state of the GUI.
 * Additional validation could occur here to insure that everything
 * is as it should be before passing the values to the database.
 *
 *
 * @return a value of type 'UnitInfo'
 */
```

```
public UnitInfo getUnitInfo() {
    UnitInfo u = new UnitInfo();
    u = current_unit;
    // this insures we pick up any non-gui items, like the db ID.
    u.setName(namefield.getText());
    u.setPartno(partnofield.getText());
    u.setSerialno(serialnofield.getText());
    try {
        u.setWeight(new Float(weightfield.getText()).floatValue());
    }
    catch (BadWeightException be) {
        displayError(be);
    }
    // grab the color and mfg db keys from the popups
    Integer I = (Integer) colorhash.get( colorcombo.getSelectedItem());
    u.setColorid(I.intValue());
    I = (Integer) mfghash.get( mfgcombo.getSelectedItem());
    u.setMfgid(I.intValue());

    return u;
}

public void setUnitInfo(UnitInfo u) {
    current_unit = u;
    namefield.setText(u.getName());
    partnofield.setText(u.getPartno());
    serialnofield.setText(u.getSerialno());
    weightfield.setText(new Float(u.getWeight()).toString());
    String popupsel = (String) mfgidhash.get(new Integer(u.getMfgid()));
    mfgcombo.setSelectedItem(popupsel);
    popupsel = (String) coloridhash.get(new Integer(u.getColorid()));
    colorcombo.setSelectedItem(popupsel);
}

public void displayError(Exception e) {
    JOptionPane.showMessageDialog(null, e);
    System.exit(1);
}


public static void main(String[] args) {
    // install a security manager if none exists
    if (System.getSecurityManager() == null) {
        System.setSecurityManager(new RMISecurityManager());
    }
```

```
JFrame f = new JFrame("The UnitDB Swing Client");
f.addWindowListener(new WindowAdapter() {
     public void windowClosing(WindowEvent e) {System.exit(0);}});

f.getContentPane().add(new UnitDbClient());
f.pack();


// centers the window in the users screen
Dimension screen = Toolkit.getDefaultToolkit().getScreenSize();
Dimension fsize = f.getSize();

// set an fixed width so that you don't take over the users screen
fsize.width=650;
fsize.height=250;
f.setSize(fsize);

f.setLocation( ( screen.width / 2 ) - ( fsize.width /2 ) ,
              ( screen.height / 2 ) - ( fsize.height /2 ) );


f.setVisible(true);

}

} // UnitDbClient
```

Note that again I have chosen to extend JPanel instead of JFrame. This gives me the flexibility to run this class standalone or as a panel in a larger application. I have also purposely avoided using anonymous inner classes when implementing listeners. I find it much easier to maintain the code with clearly defined inner classes for listeners. Others prefer to drop the class definition in the same place the GUI layout code exists and keep it all together. I've found that when maintaining code it's much simpler to keep the layout code separate and well defined, as it can get pretty messy anyway depending on what your users demand in terms of screen layout.

Note that the bulk of the code is really GUI layout based, and the actual work is done very simply and in a very modular fashion. The one trick is to make sure your methods for getting data from the GUI have the appropriate amount of error checking in them. With that done you can safely move data to and from the database. Also remember that the many layers of integrity this system provides help promote more reliability and data integrity.

Sorting Utility Functions for the GUI

The class Qsort.java was used by UnitDBClient to sort Vectors on the client side without the help of the database. If you're using a 1.2 JVM you may wish to use the Collections framework instead. However, this is a handy class to have around if you're using a 1.1 JVM.

Listing 4–4: Qsort.java

```java
import java.util.Vector;
import java.util.Date;

/**
 *  A Object sensitive quick sort algorithm for Vectors
 *
 * @author Stewart Birnam
 *
 *  This was built by hacking the QuickSort demo provided with
 *  the JDK to get the basic sorting algorithm.
 *
 *  What we changed was unhooking it from the applet gui
 *  framework. It was designed for and making it sensitive to
 *  different datatypes, i.e. Date, Number, String, Object so
 *  that those would sort properly.
 *
 *  This class sorts a index and returns it rather than actually
 *  reorder a vector, similar in the way a database indexes
 *  records.
 */

public class QSort {

    int [] index;
    Vector vec = new Vector();
    Class type;


    public QSort(Vector v) {
        vec = v;
        initIndex();
        try {
            type = Class.forName("java.lang.Object");
        }
        catch (ClassNotFoundException e) {
            // things are seriously screwed up if this happens.
            e.printStackTrace();
        }
    }
```

```
/**
 * QSort takes a vector and classtype describing what the
 *  vector contains.this insures that the vector is sorted
 *  properly.
 *
 *  the invocation would look something like this:
 *  try {
 *    QSort q = new Qsort(myvector, Class.forName("java.lang.String"));
 *  }
 *  catch (ClassNotFoundException c) { c.printStactTrace(); }
 *
 *  the exception handling is required by the forName method call.
 *
 * @param v a value of type 'Vector'
 * @param type a value of type 'Class'
 */
public QSort (Vector v, Class t) {
    vec = v;
    type = t;
    initIndex();
    sort();
}

private void initIndex() {
    index = new int[vec.size()];
    for (int i=0; i<vec.size(); i++) {
        index[i] = i;
    }
}


/**
 * The quick sort implementation, sensitive to object types.
 *  other algorithms may work faster depending on what you are
 *  doing. If you have a faster method, you can insert it into
 *  this class and call it instead of quickSort.
 * @param lo0     left boundary of the index
 * @param hi0     right boundary of the index
 */
public void quickSort( int lo0, int hi0 )
{
    int lo = lo0;
    int hi = hi0;
    Object mid;

    if ( hi0 > lo0) {

        mid =  vec.elementAt( index[( lo0 + hi0 ) / 2] );
```

```
        while( lo <= hi ) {

            int result = 0;

            Object s =  vec.elementAt(index[lo]);
            result = compareByClass(s, mid, type);

            while (( lo < hi0 ) && (result < 0) ){
                ++lo;
                s =  vec.elementAt(index[lo]);
                result = compareByClass(s, mid, type);
            }

            s = vec.elementAt(index[hi]);
            result = compareByClass(s, mid, type);

            while(( hi > lo0 ) && (  result > 0) ) {
                —hi;
                s =  vec.elementAt(index[hi]);
                result = compareByClass(s, mid, type);
            }

            if( lo <= hi ) {
                swap( lo, hi);
                ++lo;
            —hi;
            }
        }

        if( lo0 < hi ) {
            quickSort( lo0, hi);
        }

        if( lo < hi0 ) {
            quickSort( lo, hi0 );
        }
    }
}

private void swap( int i, int j) {
    int T;
    T = index[i];
    index[i] = index[j];
    index[j] = T;
}

public int compareByClass(Object obj1, Object obj2, Class type)  {

    // If both values are null return 0
    if (obj1 == null && obj2 == null) {
        return 0;
    }
```

```
else if (obj1 == null) { // Define null less than everything.
    return -1;
}
else if (obj2 == null) {
    return 1;
}

if (type.getSuperclass() == java.lang.Number.class)  {
        Number n1 = (Number) obj1;
        double d1 = n1.doubleValue();
        Number n2 = (Number) obj2;
        double d2 = n2.doubleValue();

        if (d1 < d2)
            return -1;
        else if (d1 > d2)
            return 1;
        else
            return 0;
}
else if (type == java.util.Date.class) {
        Date d1 = (Date)obj1;
        long n1 = d1.getTime();
        Date d2 = (Date)obj2;
        long n2 = d2.getTime();

        if (n1 < n2)
            return -1;
        else if (n1 > n2)
            return 1;
        else return 0;
}
else if (type == String.class) {
        String s1 = (String)obj1;
        String s2    = (String)obj2;
        int result = s1.compareTo(s2);

        if (result < 0)
            return -1;
        else if (result > 0)
            return 1;
        else return 0;
}
 else if (type == Boolean.class) {
        Boolean bool1 = (Boolean)obj1;
        boolean b1 = bool1.booleanValue();
        Boolean bool2 = (Boolean)obj2;
        boolean b2 = bool2.booleanValue();
```

```
                  if (b1 == b2)
                      return 0;
                  else if (b1) // Define false < true
                      return 1;
                  else
                      return -1;
        }
        else {
                  Object v1 = obj1;
                  String s1 = v1.toString();
                  Object v2 = obj2;
                  String s2 = v2.toString();
                  int result = s1.compareTo(s2);

                  if (result < 0)
                      return -1;
                  else if (result > 0)
                      return 1;
                  else return 0;
        }
}

public int [] sort() {
    quickSort(0, vec.size() - 1);
    return index;
}

public int [] getIndex() {
    return index;
}

public void setVector( Vector v) {
    vec = v;
    initIndex();
}

public void setType ( Class t) {
    type = t;
}

public Vector getSortedVector() {
    sort();
    int [] idx = getIndex();
    Vector nv = new Vector();
    for (int i=0; i<vec.size(); i++) {
        nv.addElement(vec.elementAt(idx[i]));
    }
    return nv;
}
```

```
*/

public class IUDPanel extends JPanel {

    public JButton insertbutton, updatebutton, deletebutton, cancelbutton;

    public IUDPanel(int orientation) {

        if (orientation != BoxLayout.X_AXIS &&
            orientation != BoxLayout.Y_AXIS) {
            orientation = BoxLayout.X_AXIS;
        }

        insertbutton = new JButton("Add");
        updatebutton = new JButton("Change");
        deletebutton = new JButton("Delete");
        cancelbutton = new JButton("Cancel");

        insertbutton.setActionCommand("INSERT");
        updatebutton.setActionCommand("UPDATE");
        deletebutton.setActionCommand("DELETE");
        cancelbutton.setActionCommand("CANCEL");

        setLayout(new BoxLayout(this, orientation));

        Dimension biggest = updatebutton.getPreferredSize();

        insertbutton.setMaximumSize(biggest);
        deletebutton.setMaximumSize(biggest);
        cancelbutton.setMaximumSize(biggest);

        add(insertbutton);
        add(updatebutton);
        add(deletebutton);
        add(Box.createVerticalGlue());
        add(cancelbutton);

    }

    public static void main(String[] args) {
        JFrame f = new JFrame();
        f.addWindowListener(new WindowAdapter() {
            public void windowClosing(WindowEvent e) {System.exit(0);}});

        f.getContentPane().add(new IUDPanel(BoxLayout.Y_AXIS));
        f.pack();
        f.show();
    }

} // IUDPanel
```

JTable as a Dynamic Database DataWindow

Building a grid-style view of database tables is a very popular idea. You can build it with the Swing class JTable, but it's fairly complex to get started. First, you'll need a datamodel that represents the contents of the grid as they relate to your database objects. For instance, a row in the grid corresponds to a record in the database, or to one of our UnitInfo Objects. Each column will need to know where to get its data from, what type it is, and how to display it.

An excellent example of using a JTable with the database actually comes with Swing. If you dig around in the examples, you'll find one called:

```
swing/examples/TableExample
```

If you poke around in there, you'll find several examples of using a JTable as a database client.

You'll find that to actually make JTable work for a relational schema can be quite a complex task, mostly due to trying to map the Model-View architecture to your schema or API. You should also keep in mind that the JTable class is a complex one and might have a bug or two in it. Consider carefully if you truly need a spreadsheet style approach to your database schema. Personally, I've found the JTable class more useful for displaying data than as an editing tool. Whatever you decide, be forewarned that you'll have a significant time investment trying to doing anything nontrivial with JTable.

Chapter 5

The Servlet as Client

Quick Start

After some background on servlet development, we illustrate how you can use
RMI from a servlet, or connect directly via JDBC. Again, the database API we
created is used in both cases. Configuration tips for Apache JServ are provided
as well.

Technology Overview

Traditionally, most programmers doing Web development don't have a lot in
common with database developers. Even though they may share the use of the
database, the difference between typical GUI/database programming issues and
Web application development usually makes it hard for the two programmers to
find common ground. In fact, they usually end up engineering their own solutions to the exact same problems.

By building a database API using Java technology, you can finally create a place where database developer and web developer meet. This has great implications beyond the fact that now both developers are using a common development language. They are now both able to leverage against the same APIs. This is of particular importance nowadays when maintaining adequate staffing can sometimes prove difficult. In the same way that you are able to transparently move hardware platforms in and out of the system (thanks to Java's Write Once Run Anywhere technology), you can now make it possible for your development staff to take on more types of projects, instead of having fixed specialties. At the very least, it should make it possible for all members of your staff to debug application problems wherever they occur. Furthermore, it should be easier to find contractors or project employees than it might be for other RAD solutions.

If you're not already using servlets, you should start. There are many resources available to teach you the ins and outs of servlet programming. However, to the uninitiated, I'll provide you an illustration and some reasons why this method will prevail over the others in the future.

Typical Web Development Scenario

Perl

Most Web programming is done with Perl and the Common Gateway Interface (CGI). CGI is a very simple way for one to write programs that interact with a Web server. A CGI program can be written in any language. That's because the Hello World program that everyone first starts with when they are learning programming is not much different from the common CGI program. Put simply, a typical CGI program takes arguments passed into it from STDIN, does some processing, and prints something to STDOUT. It's no different from any command-line program you've ever used. The only difference is that you output your text as HTML for the browser to interpret and render onto the screen. The Web server and client take care of passing the information from the STDOUT of the Web server over the network to the client.

Perl is great for writing CGI programs. It rips through text like butter, and interfaces with the Unix operating system closely, so you can have access to any system resources you need. But there are problems. First of all, there's scalability. Every time someone makes a request to run your CGI program, the Perl interpreter is loaded into RAM (~2Mb), the program is run and then exits. If many people ask for the same program, or other Perl programs simultaneously, then multiple copies of the interpreter will spawn and you may run out of RAM, start swapping, or just crash altogether.

To address this problem, several solutions have emerged to keep the interpreter resident. All of these solutions have their pitfalls. The real issue when considering Perl as a database programming language is availability of vendor database libraries for that platform. In addition, the glue between Perl and the vendor database is usually very basic, very unsupported, and not necessarily robust. However, it can be perfect for small solutions. The flexible coding style of Perl can enable you to develop very rapidly, however you usually end up with something that is not only hard to maintain, but probably has a fair amount of bugs, too.

Java

Servlets make use of a VM that is already loaded and ready to go in the Web server. Furthermore, your object is all loaded and ready to go, too. So the instantiation is just about nil. When you make a request, your object does its work. This approach scales nicely. It also lets you do things that would be very cumbersome to do in Perl, if not just plain impossible.

Most database vendors provide a Level 4 JDBC driver for their database. A Level 4 driver is implemented completely in Java. This means you don't need any platform-specific compiled libraries. All you need are the class files provided by the vendor, and you can move that to any platform with a Java VM.

Add to this the enormous amount of APIs that exist for Java in virtually every conceivable area of computer science, and you have a pretty powerful application development environment for Web applications.

Programming Concepts

Administration

Administration of a Web server that is servlet enabled is not too much different than taking care of a regular Web server. The tricky part is making sure that the CLASSPATH environment variable for the server is setup to be as lean as possible. Classes in the server's CLASSPATH will only be loaded once when the server starts up. This is fine for things that are not likely to change often, like your Oracle JDBC classes. However, if you're trying to develop something that's in the server's CLASSPATH you'll have a very difficult time as the server will cache the first invocation of that class and not see any of your recompilations!

The solution is to make use of the servlet directory that these Web servers come preconfigured for. This directory is understood by the server to contain class files that need to be reloaded when modified unless otherwise specified. If you need to install a package, you can place the package directory in this same directory. You can also configure the server to read servlets from other directories you create as well.

Support

One of the tricky things about Web development is debugging. A poorly written application will fail causing an HTTP server error and give the user or support staff little if no idea what went wrong. Typically in this instance, STDERR will be written to one of the Web server's log files. So if you know where to look, you can get a little more information about what went wrong.

One way of saving yourself the hassle of digging around trying to find the correct error log is to build a little error trapping to help yourself out. Generally, if it's an error you can anticipate, you can probably catch the exception and write it out as a Web page to the Web browser. For example, here is some code that does just that:

```java
public void httpError(Exception e,  ServletOutputStream out ) {
    try {
        out.println("<h2>Error</h2>");
        out.println("<pre>");
        out.println(e.getMessage());
        out.println("You can attempt to reconnect <a href=" +
                    SERVLET + "?reload=rmi>here</a>");
        out.println("</pre>");
    }
    catch (IOException ie) {
        log(ie.getMessage());
    }
    log(e.getMessage());
}
```

You pass your exception, as well as the ServletOutputStream, to the method. As long as you haven't done something to kill the servlet completely, your error will be printed out as a Web page, and sent to the calling browser. It will also log the error in the server's error log. If for some reason you can't write to the ServletOutputStream, that error will be logged as well.

To help yourself out even more, you can seed the exception with more information, like this:

```java
catch (RemoteException re) {
    String mymessage = "I knew this would happen. Here's why:\n" +
                    re.getMessage();
    Exception e = new Exception(mymessage);
    httpError(e, out);
}
```

A Plethora of Logs

Web servers usually have an access log and an error log. Web servers running servlets may also have additional logs for the servlets. Apache JServ, a mod for the Apache Web server that enables you to run servlets, has two additional logs, mod_jserv.log and jserv.log. Mod_jserv.log will contain servlet errors and JServ status info. Jserv.log will contain info directly from the servlets themselves. When you use the log() command, data will be written to jserv.log by default. If you don't want error messages appearing in this file, you can write to System.err, which will write to error_log. Or, you can configure JServ to use the server's main error log. Alternatively, you can simply throw a ServletException.

I prefer to use the log() method, since it not only preformats my text into Web log format—with the date format written in a manner consistent with the rest of the log—it also doesn't force a 501 or 500 error screen to appear before the user, like throwing a ServletException does. I figure that if I'm trapping an exception, then I know this is something that can go wrong. I should be able to recover gracefully or at the very least output some informative message to the user. Also, it's nice to look in one place for all my servlet activity, rather than having to merge the contents of multiple files to figure out what happened during a session.

The UnitDbServlet

This servlet is designed to provide a read-only interface to the database. It lets the user navigate through the unit hierarchy much in the same way that the JTree we built in Chapter 4 did. It does have one user input feature, however: it allows the user to upload an image file that corresponds to the currently viewed unit, and stores that image in the database as a BLOB (Binary Large Object).

Most of the details of implementing accessing BLOBS from the database and uploading files via HTTP can be found in Chapter 8. However, we'll introduce the servlets that handle this feature—namely ImageServlet and GetImageServlet—briefly in this chapter.

Using RMI from a Servlet

Accessing your remote object from a servlet is essentially the same process as it would be anywhere else. You'll want to instantiate the object in the init() method of the Servlet.

```
public void init(ServletConfig config) throws ServletException {
    super.init(config);
    initRMI();
}

public void initRMI() {
    try {
        String url = "rmi://" + RMIHOST + "/";
        unitdb = (UnitDb) Naming.lookup(url + RMINAME);
    }
```

```
    catch (Exception e) {
        log("UnitDbServlet Cannot connect to database\n");
        log(e.getMessage());
        destroy();
    }
}
```

On instantiation the Servlet calls init(). Init(), in turn calls initRMI(), which makes the actual instantiation of the remote object. RMIHOST and RMINAME are strings defined in the servlet. They could also be read in from a properties file or from an HTML Form POST operation if desired. If everything goes ok, and the reference to the remote object is successful, the servlet goes on to do its job. In the event of a failure to connect to the remote object, the servlet logs a message as well as the contents of the exception.

Handling Errors and Reconnecting to Remote Objects

Since servlets can be preloaded when the Web server starts up, there's no way to report an error to the browser on instantiation, since you may not have a browser context to report to. In this condition your only recourse is to write to the server log. However, you can handle things more gracefully in the event of a failure to connect to your remote object during a Web transaction.

For example, let's say that the servlet is invoked and everything goes ok. Then several hours later, the RMI server goes down. In a situation like this, you may have a user who has been using the servlet without a problem for a while. Now that the connection to the database has been severed, you'd like to let the user know that something has happened, rather than just failing without explanation. You can do this by first creating a method like this:

```
public void httpError(Exception e,  ServletOutputStream out ) {
    try {
        out.println("<h2>Error</h2>");
        out.println("<pre>");
        out.println(e.getMessage());
        out.println("You can attempt to reconnect <a href=" +
                SERVLET +
                "?reload=rmi>here</a>");
        out.println("</pre>");
    }
    catch (IOException ie) {
        log(ie.getMessage());
    }
    log(e.getMessage());
}
```

This method takes an exception and a ServletOutputStream as its inputs. With those, it can examine the exception, and print out a more meaningful error message to the user. In addition, this method provides the user with a link that would force the servlet to try to reconnect to the RMI server. In the doGet() method of the servlet we define an action that traps the reload=rmi key-value pair like this:

```
public void doGet (HttpServletRequest req, HttpServletResponse res)
    throws ServletException, IOException {

    String [] reload = req.getParameterValues("reload");

    if (reload != null) {
        if (reload[0].equals("rmi")) {
            initRMI();
        }
    }
}
```

This is particularly useful if your RMI server is running in a high-availability mode. As one server fails over to another, there may be a few seconds or minutes of downtime. Even if the failover completes before the remote object is used, the reference that the servlet has to the remote object is no longer valid. By providing a means for the user to force the servlet to get a new reference to the remote object, you eliminate the necessity for a tech support call. At the very least, you can make it easier for your administrators to take care of the servlet.

You use the httpError method in your exception handling like this:

```
try {
    out.println("<ul>");
    Vector v = unitdb.getChildUnits(parentid);
    if (parentid != 0 && v.size() > 0 ) {
        out.println("Contains the following units:<p>");
    }
    for (int i=0; i < v.size(); i++) {
        UnitNode u = (UnitNode) v.elementAt(i);
        out.println( "<a href=" + SERVLET +
                    "?unit_key=" + u.getId() + ">" +
                    u.getName() + "</a><br>") ;
    }
    out.println("</ul>");
}
catch (Exception re) {
    httpError(re, out);
}

}
```

When the servlet generates an exception, httpError() is called, and the result seen in Figure 5–1.

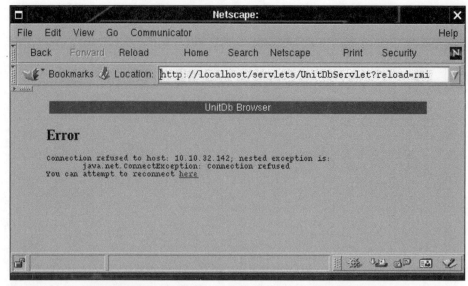

Figure 5–1: Error dialog with reconnection link, generated from httpError() method call

Accessing Your Database API from the Servlet

Once you have a reference to the remote object, using it is identical to any other context. You simply call methods on it as if it were a local object. All connectivity is handled transparently by RMI. For instance, here is a method call that draws an HTML table from the data extracted from the UnitDb API call getUnitInfo():

```
public void unitDetail(ServletOutputStream out, int id) {
  try {
      UnitInfo u = unitdb.getUnitInfo(id);
      out.println("<ul>");
      out.println("<table width=500 bgcolor=777777 cellpadding=4>");
      out.println("<tr><td align=right>" + fontize("Name:") + "</td>");
      out.println("<td>" +fontize(u.getName()) + "</td>");
      if (u.getParentname() == null) { u.setParentname("Top");}
      out.println("<td><a href=" + SERVLET + "?unit_key=" +
              u.getParentid() + ">" +
              fontize("Return to: " +
              u.getParentname()) + "</a></td></tr>");

      out.println("<tr><td align=right>" +
      fontize("Part No:") + "</td><td>" + fontize(u.getPartno()) +
      "</td><td rowspan=5 align=center valign=middle>" +
      "<img src=\"/servlets/GetImageServlet?unitid=" + u.getId() +
      "\"><br>Upload a new image " +
      "<a href=/servlets/ImageServlet?unitid=" + u.getId() +
```

```
            ">here</a></td></tr>");
            out.println("<tr><td align=right>" + fontize("Serial No:") +
            "</td><td>" + fontize(u.getSerialno()) + "</td></tr>");
            out.println("<tr><td align=right>" + fontize("Weight:") +
            "</td><td>" + fontize("" + u.getWeight()) + "</td></tr>");
            out.println("<tr><td align=right>" + fontize("Color:") +
            "</td><td>" +
            fontize((String)coloridhash.get(new Integer(u.getColorid()))) +
            "</td></tr>");
            out.println("<tr><td align=right>" + fontize("Mfg:") +
            "</td><td>" +
            fontize((String)mfgidhash.get(new Integer(u.getMfgid()))) +
            "</td></tr>");
            out.println("</table>");
            out.println("</ul>");
        }
        catch (Exception re) {
            httpError(re, out);
        }


    }
```

Accessing Your API Locally

You may have noticed a call to another servlet in the above example, ImageServlet. This servlet uses the UnitDbImpl object directly rather than as a remote reference. This is done mostly for performance purposes, as we don't want to tie up our remote object's database connection with potentially long file uploads.

An alternative to accessing the object locally would be to publish another remote object using the UnitDBServer object and passing in a different name for the RMI object in the registry. This may be a better alternative, as making an instance of the UnitDbImpl class directly means having access to the Oracle classes on the Web server's classpath. And obviously you'll need to install the Oracle classes on the Web server, whereas with the RMI approach that wouldn't be necessary as RMI is part of the core Java API.

Configuring Apache JServ for Oracle JDBC Access

Adding the classpath is not too difficult. Edit the jserv.properties file, which in a standard installation of Apache JServ would be found in:

```
path_to_apache/conf/jserv/jserv.properties
```

Find the wrapper.classpath entries and add the Oracle classes. You can have as many wrapper.classpath entries as you need.

```
wrapper.classpath=/usr/local/apache/libexec/ApacheJServ.jar
wrapper.classpath=/usr/local/JSDK2.0
wrapper.classpath=/usr/local/oracle/jdbc/lib/classes111.zip
```

Now you need to restart the Web server so that JServ can see the new classpath. Again, by using RMI you would not need the classpath addition, additional software, or have to restart the server. Choosing which method you end up using will be based on how fast your Web servers are vs. your RMI servers, and the average load upon them. Experimentation will be necessary to determine the best combination for your environment.

If you're using Apache with Java 2, you can place the Oracle classes in your `$JAVA_HOME/jre/lib/ext` directory, and then they will be included automatically without a specific reference in your CLASSPATH.

Using JDBC from a Servlet

GetImageServlet extracts BLOBS directly from the database, sets the content type to image/jpeg, and then streams the image to the browser. Since the amount of data that gets extracted from the database might be very large, it makes sense to let this servlet have its own database connection rather than sharing the connection already used by the UnitDb remote object.

Another issue is that for this particular application, we are streaming binary data back to the Web browser. In order to make this happen out of RMI, you'd have to pass something serializable, like an image object. So, you'd have to connect to the database, read the bits into an image, and once done, then send the image object back to the servlet, which would have to deconstruct it and spray out the bits again. Not very efficient.

So, in this case we connect directly to the database via JDBC. Again, in order to make this happen you'll first have to configure JServ to see the Oracle classes as detailed above.

The rest is straightforward. The connection is accomplished the same way it was done for the UnitDbImpl class, except that it happens in the init() method of the servlet.

```
public class GetImageServlet extends HttpServlet {

    Connection conn;
    String url;

    public void init(ServletConfig config) throws ServletException {
      // setup the db connectionyes
      super.init(config);

      try {
          DriverManager.registerDriver (new oracle.jdbc.driver.OracleDriver ());
          // hard code the hostname and user/pass for now...
          url = "jdbc:oracle:thin:@localhost:1521:book";
```

```
            conn = DriverManager.getConnection (url, "stewartb", "stewartb");
            log("connected: " + conn);
    }
    catch (SQLException se) { log(se.getMessage()); }
}
```

With the connection object now global and instantiated, you can make JDBC calls directly within your servlet.

A complete description of the GetImageServlet and the ImageServlet is in Chapter 8.

Combining All Three Methods to Build a Web Application

The UnitDbServlet, GetImageServlet, and ImageServlet are all combined to produce our illustrative Web application. This application allows us to browse our Oracle unit database, view images of each of the units, and upload new images to the database. For now we'll focus on the workings of the UnitDbServlet, and save the ImageServlet and GetImageServlet for Chapter 8.

If the servlet is called with no query string or posted form data, it produces the screen shown in Figure 5–2.

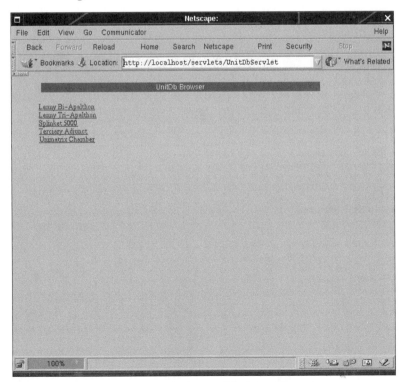

Figure 5–2: Opening screen of the UnitDbServlet

```
public void doGet (HttpServletRequest req, HttpServletResponse res)
    throws ServletException, IOException {
    ServletOutputStream out = res.getOutputStream();
    res.setContentType("text/html");
    out.println(printHeader());
    String [] uk = req.getParameterValues("unit_key");
    String [] reload = req.getParameterValues("reload");

    if (reload != null) {
        if (reload[0].equals("rmi")) {
            initRMI();
        }
    }

    if ( uk == null) {
        printUnits(out, 0);
    } else {
        if (!uk[0].equals("0")) {
            unitDetail(out,  new Integer(uk[0]).intValue());
        }
        for (int i = 0; i < uk.length; i++) {
            printUnits(out, new Integer(uk[i]).intValue() );
        }
    }

    out.close();
}
```

As you can see from the doGet() method, if the string array sk is null, then the printUnits method is called passing in the default database id of 0. This will force a listing of all the "parent"records in the database, as they are all children of the "seed" record with the ID of 0. Hence, calling the servlet without arguments gets us to this starting point.

Clicking on one of the links takes us to the screen shown in Figure 5–3.

Having clicked on one of the links, we are passing in a unit_key number to the servlet, which in turn does a method call on our UnitDb database API. The unitDetail method (listed above) calls the UnitDb.getUnitInfo method and then renders the result of the call as HTML. Then the servlet calls the printUnits method again, passing in the ID for this unit, thus getting a listing of any child units. A link is also provided to navigate up the tree to the parent unit. A link is also provided for the user to upload a new picture for this unit. Again, see Chapter 8 for more information on file uploads, BLOBS, and binary streams from the database.

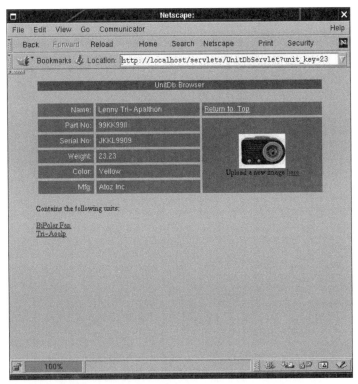

Figure 5–3: A record from the UnitDB database displayed by the UnitDbServlet

Here is the complete listing of the UnitDbServlet:

Listing 5–1: UnitDbServlet.java

```java
import java.io.*;
import javax.servlet.*;
import javax.servlet.http.*;
import java.rmi.*;
import java.util.*;

/**
 * UnitDbServlet.java
 *
 *
 * Created: Thu Nov 11 17:33:19 1999
 *
```

```
 * @author Stewart Birnam
 * @version 1.0
 */

public class UnitDbServlet extends HttpServlet {
    /*----------------------------------------------------------------*
     *   GLOBALS
    /*----------------------------------------------------------------*/

    String url;
    String RMINAME = "UNITDB";
    String RMIHOST = "drdoom";
    // our handle on the RMI object
    UnitDb unitdb;
    // our URL for self-referral
    String SERVLET = "/servlets/UnitDbServlet";
    // hashtables to store frequently accessed information
    Hashtable colorhash, mfghash, coloridhash, mfgidhash;

    public void init(ServletConfig config) throws ServletException {
        super.init(config);
        initRMI();
        loadHash();
    }


    public void initRMI() {
        try {
            String url = "rmi://" + RMIHOST + "/";
            unitdb = (UnitDb) Naming.lookup(url + RMINAME);
        }
        catch (Exception e) {
            log("UnitDbServlet Cannot connect to database\n");
            log(e.getMessage());
            destroy();
        }
    }

    public void loadHash() {
        try {
            colorhash = unitdb.getColor();
            mfghash = unitdb.getMfg();
            coloridhash = new Hashtable();
            mfgidhash = new Hashtable();
            Object obj;
            for (Enumeration e = colorhash.keys(); e.hasMoreElements();){
                obj = e.nextElement();
                coloridhash.put(colorhash.get(obj), obj);
            }
```

```
            for (Enumeration e = mfghash.keys(); e.hasMoreElements();) {
                obj = e.nextElement();
                mfgidhash.put(mfghash.get(obj), obj);
            }
        }
    catch (RemoteException re) {
            log("UnitDbServlet Cannot connect to database\n");
            log(re.getMessage());
            destroy();
        }
}


public void doGet (HttpServletRequest req, HttpServletResponse res)
    throws ServletException, IOException {
    ServletOutputStream out = res.getOutputStream();

    // set content type and other response header fields first
    res.setContentType("text/html");
    out.println(printHeader());
    String [] uk = req.getParameterValues("unit_key");
    String [] reload = req.getParameterValues("reload");

    if (reload != null) {
        if (reload[0].equals("rmi")) {
            initRMI();
        }
    }


/*-----------------------------------------------------------*
 *  we got multiple values for unit_key?
/*-----------------------------------------------------------*/

    if ( uk == null) {
        printUnits(out, 0);
    } else {
        if (!uk[0].equals("0")) {
            unitDetail(out,  new Integer(uk[0]).intValue());
        }
        for (int i = 0; i < uk.length; i++) {
            printUnits(out, new Integer(uk[i]).intValue() );
        }
    }

    out.close();
}
```

```java
public void printUnits(ServletOutputStream out, int parentid) {
    try {
        out.println("<ul>");
        Vector v = unitdb.getChildUnits(parentid);
        if (parentid != 0 && v.size() > 0 ) {
            out.println("Contains the following units:<p>");
        }
        for (int i=0; i < v.size(); i++) {
            UnitNode u = (UnitNode) v.elementAt(i);
            out.println( "<a href=" + SERVLET + "?unit_key=" + u.getId() +
            ">" + u.getName() + "</a><br>") ;
        }
        out.println("</ul>");
    }
    catch (RemoteException re) {
        httpError(re, out);
    }
    catch (IOException ie) {
        httpError(ie, out);
    }
}


/**
 * unitDetail extracts all the pertinent data from the
 * UnitInfo object that it retrieves from
 * the unitdb object, and writes it out as a HTML table.
 *
 * @param out a value of type 'ServletOutputStream'
 * @param id a value of type 'int'
 */
public void unitDetail(ServletOutputStream out, int id) {
    try {
        UnitInfo u = unitdb.getUnitInfo(id);
        out.println("<ul>");
        out.println("<table width=500 bgcolor=777777 cellpadding=4>");
        out.println("<tr><td align=right>" + fontize("Name:") + "</td>");
        out.println("<td>" +fontize(u.getName()) + "</td>");
        if (u.getParentname() == null) { u.setParentname("Top"); }
        out.println("<td><a href=" + SERVLET + "?unit_key=" +
        u.getParentid() + ">" +
        fontize("Return to: " + u.getParentname()) + "</a></td></tr>");
        out.println("<tr><td align=right>"+ fontize("Part No:") +
        "</td><td>" + fontize(u.getPartno()) +
        "</td><td rowspan=5 align=center valign=middle>" +
        "<img src=\"/servlets/GetImageServlet?unitid=" + u.getId() +
        "\"><br>Upload a new image <a href=/servlets/ImageServlet?unitid=" +
        u.getId() + ">here</a></td></tr>");
        out.println("<tr><td align=right>" + fontize("Serial No:") +
        "</td><td>" + fontize(u.getSerialno()) + "</td></tr>");
```

```
        out.println("<tr><td align=right>" + fontize("Weight:") + "</td><td>" +
        fontize("" + u.getWeight()) + "</td></tr>");
        out.println("<tr><td align=right>" + fontize("Color:") + "</td><td>" +
        fontize((String)coloridhash.get(new Integer(u.getColorid()))) +
        "</td></tr>");
        out.println("<tr><td align=right>" + fontize("Mfg:") + "</td><td>" +
        fontize((String)mfgidhash.get(new Integer(u.getMfgid()))) + "</td></tr>");
        out.println("</table>");
        out.println("</ul>");
    }
    catch (Exception re) {
        httpError(re, out);
    }

}

public String getServletInfo() {
    return "The UnitDb servlet";
}

public String printHeader() {
    String s = "<ul><table width=500 bgcolor=555555>" +
        "<tr><td align=center>" + fontize("UnitDb Browser") + "</td></tr>" +
        "</table></ul>";
    return s;
}

public String fontize(String s) {
    return "<font face=helvetica color=f4f4f4>" + s + "</font>";
}

/**
 * This method will report any errors directly to the web browser, rather than
 * ending up in a server log somewhere. Very useful for debugging and handling
 * errors that we can predict.
 *
 * Notice that you can also allow the user to make method calls by providing
 * links that pass back in values you can act on. The link printed in the
 * method would force the servlet to reinitalize
 * it's RMI object by calling initRMI() from doGet().
 *
 * @param e a value of type 'Exception'
 * @param out a value of type 'ServletOutputStream'
 */
```

```
public void httpError(Exception e,  ServletOutputStream out ) {
    try {
        out.println("<h2>Error</h2>");
        out.println("<pre>");
        out.println(e.getMessage());
        out.println("You can attempt to reconnect <a href=" +
        SERVLET + "?reload=rmi>here</a>");
        out.println("</pre>");
    }
    catch (IOException ie) {
        log(ie.getMessage());
    }
    log(e.getMessage());
}
}
```

Chapter **6**

The Command-Line Client—Providing Simplified Access to Your Database API

▼ Quick Start

▼ Technology Overview

▼ Programming Techniques

▼ Providing Data Export Services to StarOffice, Excel, Filemaker, and Other Applications

▼ Passing in TAB from the Command Line

▼ Using Unix Tools to Enhance Output and Save You Coding Time

▼ Sending Mail with sendmail

▼ Wrapping Things Up Nicely with GetOpts

▼ Conclusion

Quick Start

This chapter covers building a command-line client. It shows how you can use Java to do things you might do with C or Perl on a Unix system. Again, we use the database API we created, and show how one can parse or filter text in a way familiar to Unix users and sysadmins. We also cover how to make your database API generate text importable by spreadsheet programs like StarOffice and Excel.

Technology Overview

Don't skip over this chapter! Many developers today think of the command line as something archaic. However, with the growing popularity of open source operating systems like Linux, a whole new wave of command-line advocates are being born. Part of this is also being fueled by a surge of entry-level programmers discovering Perl, CGI, and HTML. Suddenly, thanks to the Web, ASCII text can generate a GUI by means of HTML. This means that more and more people are munging text like never before.

115

Providing a command-line text interface to your API means you can open up your system to people who would otherwise not have the time or inclination to understand it. All they need to know is that they can pass in certain values to your program and get out some predictable formatted text. This they can parse and use in their own systems. In effect, you've provided a means by which less-skilled developers can contribute to integrating your system into other systems, as well as building custom reporting mechanisms for you.

Bear in mind that from time to time people may want brief and simple results from your system. They may not be interested in launching a full GUI to get a small amount of information. Others may want to extract information from your system to drive parts of their system (which may not be written in Java). The bottom line is that providing this kind of interface makes the information you're trying to distribute available to everyone, particularly those wanting to build their own interfaces and systems in other languages.

Programming Techniques

Let's say that the legacy system you're replacing used to provide a text listing of all the units of a particular color. It would be simple to write some SQL as follows:

```
select unit.id, unit.parentid, unit.name, unit.partno, unit.serialno,
       unit.weight, unit.color, unit.mfg, unit.mdate, unit.cdate
from unit, color
where unit.color = color.id and
       lower(color.name) = '$my_color'
```

...and be done with it. However, in order to talk to the database directly this way, even with a script, you need to have the vendor database client software installed on every client. Furthermore, all your users will need accounts in the database, etc. We were trying to avoid all that.

The solution is to build a simple reporting method that takes information from the API and formats the data into printable text rather than populating a GUI or Web page with values. In our API we already have a method as follows:

```
public Vector findColor(String s) throws RemoteException
```

In our client, we can call this method and format a nice delimited string that outputs to STDOUT.

```
public void findByColor(String c) {
   try {
       Vector v = unitdb.findColor(c);
       UnitInfo u;
       System.out.println("ID:NAME:PARTNO:SERIALNO:WEIGHT");
       for (int i=0; i< v.size(); i++) {
         u = (UnitInfo) v.elementAt(i);
         System.out.println(u.getId() + delimiter +
```

```
                    u.getName() + delimiter +
                    u.getPartno() + delimiter +
                    u.getSerialno() + delimiter +
                    u.getWeight()
                    );
            }
        }
    catch (Exception e) {
            System.err.println("An error occurred while printing the text");
            System.err.println(e.getMessage());
    }
}
```

Providing Data Export Services to StarOffice, Excel, Filemaker, and Other Applications

Another use of a text interface is to provide data interchange between your system and other applications. One common scenario is for managers to want to extract data from your system to use in their spreadsheets or reports. It also provides you a mechanism for them to use the data to do forecasting or make graphs. (Although you could write your own graphing package in Java!)

In our class, we have a method to set the delimiter to whatever string we desire. This lets us change the delimiter at runtime by passing in a -Dunitdb.delimiter= value. So if you wanted to pull this data into a spreadsheet for modeling, you could set the delimiter to the TAB character, which programs such as Excel, Filemaker, and others support as a data interchange format. Or you could set the delimiter to the : character (the default), which many command-line filters in Unix understand by default.

Passing in TAB from the Command Line

It's often difficult to pass in nonprintable characters at the command line. To make things simpler, we've coded our setDelimiter method as follows:

```
public void setDelimiter(String d) {
    if (d.equals("TAB")) {
        d = "\t";
    }
    delimiter = d;
}
```

Now we can call the program from the command line like this:

```
java -Dunitdb.delimiter=TAB -Dunitdb.color=yellow UnitDbCmdLin > import_file
```

and the output of the program will go to a file that can later be imported to StarOffice, Excel, or Filemaker. See Figure 6–1.

	A	B	C	D	E	F	G	H	I
1	ID	NAME	PARTNO	SERIALNO	WEIGHT				
2	23	Lenny Tri-Apalthon	99KK99ll	JKKL9909	23.23				
3	26	BiPolar Fan	5634	N32	3.23				
4	29	Plomtk Torus	4441	N342	43.23				
5	31	Blomphix	7221	N32	6.21				
6	32	BiPolar Fan	4261	N32	3.53				
7	33	TriPolar Fan	3231	N32	35.5				
8	34	Zeelum	4881	N32	2.23				
9	35	Naxuifx	6631	N32	2.78				
10	36	teedle	5531	N32	3.13				

Figure 6–1: import_file imported into StarOffice spreadsheet

Using Unix Tools to Enhance Output and Save You Coding Time

Using the default delimiter of : we get the following output:

```
ID:NAME:PARTNO:SERIALNO:WEIGHT
23:Lenny Tri-Apalthon:99KK9911:JKKL9909:23.23
26:BiPolar Fan:5634:N32:3.23
29:Plomtk Torus:4441:N342:43.23
31:Blomphix:7221:N32:6.21
32:BiPolar Fan:4261:N32:3.53
33:TriPolar Fan:3231:N32:35.5
34:Zeelum:4881:N32:2.23
35:Naxuifx:6631:N32:2.78
36:teedle:5531:N32:3.13
```

This is perfect for parsing by Perl or another program but it doesn't look very pretty. Perhaps you just wanted to read the output. All you have to do now is pipe the output of your program to existing filters present in Unix to get pretty, printable output.

```
> java -Dunitdb.color=yellow UnitDbCmdLin | pr -e:20


1999-12-30 11:05                               Page     1


 ID    NAME                    PARTNO       SERIALNO    WEIGHT
 23    Lenny Tri-Apalthon      99KK9911     JKKL9909     23.23
 26    BiPolar Fan             5634         N32           3.23
 29    Plomtk Torus            4441         N342         43.23
 31    Blomphix                7221         N32           6.21
 32    BiPolar Fan             4261         N32           3.53
 33    TriPolar Fan            3231         N32          35.5
 34    Zeelum                  4881         N32           2.23
 35    Naxuifx                 6631         N32           2.78
 36    teedle                  5531         N32           3.13
```

PR is a tool for formatting text into printable columnar output. By inserting other filters like CUT, GREP, and SORT you can further change the output in any way desirable. Your users can decide to do whatever they want, just as they would with any command-line program in Unix.

Sending Mail with sendmail

Having the text interface lets you do many things quickly. You could even send the text formatted above by piping it directly to sendmail.

```
> java -Dunitdb.color=yellow UnitDbCmdLin | pr -e:20 |\
    /usr/lib/sendmail -t kodos@altair.com
```

Of course you can make use of the excellent JavaMail API, but if you're in a rush, this can get you there while you finish integrating JavaMail. JavaMail has the distinct advantage of being fully cross-platform, while tricks like piping to sendmail are strictly Unix.

Wrapping Things Up Nicely with GetOpts

While you've taken care of things neatly for your script programmers and "power users," you still need a way for the average user to use these programs as well. After a spell, even your power users will start asking for a more complete offering.

Unix shell scriptors are long familiar with getopts. If you're not familiar with getopts, it is a library for parsing command-line options. It provides you with a standardized and simplified way of handling these options in your code, saving you the trouble of what is usually not an exciting programming exercise.

We've already built our program to accept values for the color and delimiter. In addition, we'll let people specify a filename as well. A shell script to do this would look like this:

Listing 6–1: unitreport

```sh
#!/bin/sh
TEMP=`getopt -o c:d:f:  - "$@"`
JAVA_HOME=/usr/java
CLASSPATH=$JAVA_HOME/lib/classes.zip:.

eval set - "$TEMP"

while true ; do
    case "$1" in
    -c)
        PROPS="$PROPS -Dunitdb.color=$2"
        shift 2
          ;;
    -f)
        FILE="> $2"
        shift 2
          ;;
    -d)
         PROPS="$PROPS -Dunitdb.delimiter=$2"
         shift 2
          ;;
    -h)
         echo "unitreport [-c color] [-d delimiter] [-f file]"
         exit 0
          ;;
    -) shift ; break ;;
    *) echo "Internal error!" ; exit 1 ;;
    esac
done

eval $JAVA_HOME/bin/java $PROPS UnitDbCmdLin $FILE
```

Our script takes four possible values: -h, -c , -f, and -d. This allows us to specify the values in a manner consistent with other Unix programs. It also lets us set up the Java environment for the user in case they don't have one already. So, for instance:

```sh
unitreport -c blue -d %%% -f bluereport
```

will print out all blue units, delimited by "%%%" to a file called bluereport.

Getopts is also available for Java. It allows you to parse command-line options in the same way the shell script does. You can find it and other useful classes at *www.gnu.org*.

Conclusion

Now your users can model and format the data in any way they desire, and include it in their reports and communications. You've also opened up your system to those without the time or inclination to learn Java. However, you've done it in an easy to understand way that you can control. It may be much easier to get your Web developer to write a wrapper Perl script around the unitreport command than it would be to wait for them to learn to program servlets to your API. Certainly this may not be the most efficient means available, but it is a way for you to provide information simply to users and to legacy applications. It may also just be necessary to smooth the edges and speed up getting your system accepted by the organization's many differing programming factions.

The complete source code follows.

Listing 6–2: UnitDbCmdLin.java

```java
import java.util.*;
import java.rmi.*;

/**
 * UnitDbCmdLin.java
 *
 *
 * Created: Wed Dec 29 22:58:15 1999
 *
 * @author (c) 1999, 2000 Stewart Birnam
 * @version 1.0
 */

public class UnitDbCmdLin {

    UnitDb unitdb;
    String delimiter = ":";

    public UnitDbCmdLin() {
        initRMI("localhost", "UNITDB");
    }

    public UnitDbCmdLin(String rmihost, String rminame) {
        initRMI(rmihost, rminame);
    }

    public void initRMI(String rmihost,  String rminame) {
        try {
            String url = "rmi://" + rmihost + "/";
            unitdb = (UnitDb) Naming.lookup(url + rminame);
        }
```

```
        catch (Exception e) {
            System.err.println("Cannot connect to database\n");
            System.err.println(e.getMessage());
            System.exit(1);
        }
    }

    public void setDelimiter(String d) {
        if (d.equals("TAB")) {
            d = "\t";
        }
        delimiter = d;
    }

    public void findByColor(String c) {
        try {
            Vector v = unitdb.findColor(c);
            UnitInfo u;
            System.out.println("ID" + delimiter +
                    "NAME" + delimiter +
                    "PARTNO" + delimiter +
                    "SERIALNO" + delimiter + "WEIGHT");
            for (int i=0; i< v.size(); i++) {
                u = (UnitInfo) v.elementAt(i);
                System.out.println(u.getId() + delimiter +
                    u.getName() + delimiter +
                    u.getPartno() + delimiter +
                    u.getSerialno() + delimiter +
                    u.getWeight()
                    );
            }
        }
        catch (Exception e) {
            System.err.println("An error has occurred formatting the text");
            System.err.println(e.getMessage());
        }
    }

    public static void main(String[] args) {
        UnitDbCmdLin u;

        // check for properties
        Properties p = System.getProperties();
        String rminame = p.getProperty("unitdb.rminame");
        String hostname = p.getProperty("unitdb.hostname");
        String color = p.getProperty("unitdb.color");
        String delimiter = p.getProperty("unitdb.delimiter");

        if (rminame != null && hostname != null) {
            u = new UnitDbCmdLin(hostname, rminame);
        } else {
```

```
            u = new UnitDbCmdLin();
        }

        if (delimiter != null) {
            u.setDelimiter(delimiter);
        }

        if (color != null) {
            u.findByColor(color);
        } else {
            System.out.println("No color specified. Running " +
                    "test routine... finding for color: yellow");
            u.findByColor("yellow");
        }
        System.exit(0);
    }

} // UnitDbCmdLin
```

Distribution

Quick Start

This chapter covers deployment of your software, and suggests a number of ways that work particularly well in an intranet.

Technology Overview

Sometimes the most daunting part of any development project is actual deployment. This is particularly true with database applications. Usually, the client has to be preinstalled with the database vendor's client libraries as well as the actual application binaries. In the case of development using an interpreted language (Java), the interpreter must be installed and properly configured. Finally, your software must be installed on the client as well. All these installations require their own environment and dependencies to run properly. Layering them on top of each other makes for a delicate balance of software for stable functionality.

Getting all this to work properly is difficult and time-consuming. Each piece of software has different requirements for installation. Installing it requires knowledge of the host operating system and configuration, expertise with the various packages, and how their respective installers behave. Combined with this is the fact that you may be taking up a significant amount of disk space on the user's machine when the installation is complete.

Further difficulties emerge as new releases of the various layers arrive on the scene. Incompatibilities may emerge between the various layers. Installation problems may cause multiple versions to be concurrently on the same machine, causing conflicts and other stability issues.

With the availability of inexpensive LANs running 100baseT, and some well-known protocols, it's now possible to solve these issues for internal deployment in an organization. Let's consider the following services:

- NFS—A protocol for sharing files among (typically Unix) workstations.

- FTP—A protocol for doing efficient, authenticated file transfers over a network.

- HTTP—A very well-known protocol for delivering data over a network in a stateless manner.

- Samba—An implementation of a PC-based file sharing system used on Win32 Platforms. Samba enables Unix servers to emulate an NT file server.

What we are going to do is create a repository for our software. From this repository, we will make accessible everything the clients and servers will need to run our application. It will be available from a number of different protocols, so that whatever platform the client runs in, they will have some kind of access to the software (see Figure 7–1).

Now it may seem like overkill to have all these services accessing the same data. Depending on your environment and needs this may very well be true. However, let's consider the differences between the protocols first, and then you can decide which methods will be best for your system.

Network Disk Space: Application Servers with NFS and Samba

Let's consider the problem above: getting the software installed properly on all our client workstations. Remember that all the components of the software package—vendor binaries, interpreters, class files, etc.—are all read-only to the user. In fact, it makes the system more stable if the end-user can't delete parts of the software accidentally or in an effort to create more free local disk space. In most applications, the software gets loaded into RAM once on invocation, and has very few if any disk reads after that, with the exception perhaps of writing user data to local disk. In a distributed database application, all data would most likely be written to the database, so there would be no local disk access at all.

If I were to setup a directory on a file server, and install my JVM and class files there, along with whatever support software and files they needed, I could then have my clients mount that drive and run the software from that drive. No individual workstation installation, all clients have the same exact software, and all updates can now happen simultaneously.

You can even keep multiple versions of the JVM installed on your server, and invoke the correct one through shell scripts or batch files. You can also store your various Unix JVMs (Solaris, Linux, Win32, etc.) on the same server as well. So you can keep all your client's JVM installations centrally located and properly configured.

As long as you have a reasonably fast LAN, you should not incur too much of a penalty loading the VM and your classes over the Net. Furthermore, the tremendous savings in ease of administration and deployment easily outweigh a few extra seconds of application load time.

Stateless File Serving with HTTP

It may turn out that you either have clients that may not be able to either NFS mount or Samba mount. If some of your clients are on Macintoshes, you could try to install a commercial NFS client for Macs or use WebNFS. However, the installation of these can be a bit tricky, and you then need to deal with your Mac users having Unix login accounts, in order to validate themselves to the NFS server. This may not be desirable. In that event, a far simpler solution is to simply download whatever class files are needed via HTTP by having a bootstrap program install them for you. This is also a great way to do software updates.

Setting Up Your Server for Multiple Protocol Access

The trick now is to reconfigure these services, which typically serve up different directories off the server to all point to the same directory, which we will call for purposes of our example, /deploy.

A Suggested Directory Structure

/deploy/java contains the JVM's for the different platforms we are deploying on. Each subdirectory contains a complete JDK or JRE for that platform, with all the extra features you might require installed. (Extra features like Swing, Oracle classes, JavaMail, etc.)

/deploy/classes contains your Java classes or packages, organized in some way that makes your life easy. If you are using packages, then the organization is largely taken care of for you.

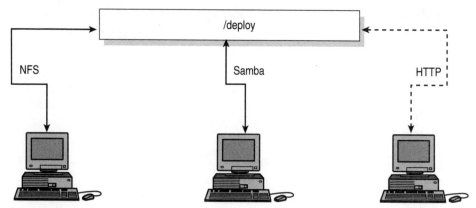

Figure 7-1: Distributing your Java classes via multiple protocols from a single server

`/deploy/bin` contains shell scripts and MSDOS batch files for launching your applications. These scripts also configure the user's environment for you, setting JAVA_HOME, CLASSPATH, and PATH so that you don't have to worry about the user's environment or software installation.

Let's now setup our application for deployment under this system, building what we need along the way.

Deploying via NFS/Samba

Regardless of which protocol you use, you're essentially doing the same thing. All your class files and, if desired, your JVM lie on a file server. When the user wants to run the application, they mount the server and run the application. The client CPU loads the application in the same way it would off a local disk. The only difference is that the software distribution is maintained at a central location.

Deploying to Unix Clients via NFS

The first step is to create the usual shell script to start your Java application. The only real difference is that you will be pointing to software that lives in NFS space, rather than locally. Here's an example script:

```
#!/bin/sh
TEMP='getopt -o c:d:f:h  — "$@"'
JAVA_HOME=/net/ourfileserver/java
CLASSPATH=$JAVA_HOME/lib/classes.zip:.
DEPLOY=/net/ourfileserver/deploy

#cd to nfs class file location
cd $DEPLOY
```

```
eval set — "$TEMP"

while true ; do
    case "$1" in
 -c)
    PROPS="$PROPS -Dunitdb.color=$2"
    shift 2
      ;;
 -f)
    FILE="> $2"
    shift 2
      ;;
 -d)
    PROPS="$PROPS -Dunitdb.delimiter=$2"
    shift 2
      ;;
 -h)
    echo "unitreport [-c color] [-d delimiter] [-f file]"
    exit 0
      ;;
 —) shift ; break ;;
 *) echo "Internal error!" ; exit 1 ;;
    esac
done
```

```
eval $JAVA_HOME/bin/java $PROPS UnitDbCmdLin $FILE
```

Now comes the chicken and the egg portion. How do I start things up? In a
Unix environment you have several choices how to bootstrap this process.

1.   You can distribute a simple shell script to all your workstations that
      invokes the script on the file server. This has the added advantage that it
      can do a small amount of error checking and notify the user if for some
      reason you can't mount the file server.

2.   You can make a symbolic link in the user's path on all workstations to
      point to the script on the file server.

3.   You can create an alias in each user's environment that points to the net-
      work script.

Deploying to Win32 Clients via Samba

This scenario is very similar to deploying over NFS, however you need to make
DOS batch files rather than shell scripts. This can prove a bit daunting, as finding adequate documentation on batch files can be difficult these days. Also, in
this environment you have to dynamically mount the file server and remember
to unmount when you finish. An example DOS batch file that does this looks
like this:

```
net use x: \\samba.krell.com\deploy
x:
cd x:\lib\unitdb
set CLASSPATH=x:\bin\jdk1.1.8\lib\classes.zip;.;x:\bin\jdk1.1.8\lib\swingall.jar
x:\bin\jdk1.1.6\bin\java UnitDbClient
```

If you want to be extra clever, you can place this batch file on the server, mount it from your Win32 workstation, make a shortcut to it, and then e-mail the short-cut to your users. If they can figure out how to install the shortcut on their desktop, then your software is deployed. Otherwise, you'll have to make a one-time visit to install the shortcut for them.

Deploying to Any Client via HTTP

This is assuming that any kind of file-sharing scenario outlined above is out of the question. You can easily distribute your classes by using the jar command. For instance, you could wrap up all your class files by changing to the directory where they live and typing:

```
jar -cf myclasses.jar *.class
```

Putting this file in a well-known URL would make it accessible to your users for download onto their desktops. That along with a shell script/batch file to launch it for them, of course.

Updating Unix Clients via NFS and Win32 Clients via Samba

Simple. Just copy your new classes/software to the file server and you're done. The next time someone launches the application they'll have the latest version.

Updating Any Client via HTTP

You could make your client connect to the URL that points to your new jar file at startup and check to see if the file is newer than the one it already has. If it is, it could download the file without user intervention and then popup a dialog telling the user to restart the program.

Conclusion

It may not be possible to build a distribution scheme like this in your environment. There may be security issues you can't overcome (probably due to political or resource-availability issues) that prohibit you from having your clients net-mount to read your software. However, you can probably argue the time invested having support staff maintaining software distributions out in the field outweighs the cost of having users utilize a central resource for software. Application servers are not a new concept, and it's one that is going to become more attractive to more organizations as the cost of administrators continues to climb. In any event, making use of some of the techniques described above should at least make your life easier and your software more manageable as your system develops.

Chapter **8**

Reading and Writing Multimedia Content, Database BLOBS, and Web-based Binary Content Delivery

- ▼ Load Balancing Between Objects
- ▼ Metadata
- ▼ Adding BLOB Support in the API and Implementation
- ▼ Web-based Binary Content Delivery
- ▼ Uploading Files
- ▼ A Servlet for Uploading Pictures
- ▼ A Servlet Displaying Pictures
- ▼ Code Listings

Quick Start

This chapter shows you how to use the Oracle database as a file system via use of BLOBs (Binary Large Objects) to store jpeg images used in your dynamically database-driven Web application. Specifically, we will show how to upload files via HTTP, update the database with new image data, and deliver BLOB data from the database to a Web browser.

Technology Overview

Many database vendors today seem to be expanding their offerings to make the database the cornerstone of your computing infrastructure. Some of the literature suggests that you should actually replace the filesystem with the database by storing all your content and metadata within it.

This is attractive in one regard if you've invested a great deal in the database already. Utilizing it in broader ways may seem to be better cost justification, particularly in instances where you have so many files to manage that it might be too cumbersome using traditional methods. Alternatively, stuffing large amounts of data in the database may impose additional costs in terms of storage and backup requirements. If you're trying to keep a database up and running 24/7 you may not want to unnecessarily increase the amount of time it takes you to export the database or back it up. Furthermore, there may be scalability issues depending on the size of the individual files you're storing in the database.

There are certain applications, particularly Web-driven applications, where it is convenient to store binary content in the database. For one thing, it saves you from having to synchronize the file system with the database metadata. Database replication tools can be used to mirror content among multiple servers. You can also consolidate your security with whatever mechanism you use to authenticate to the database, rather than authenticating to the file system as well and keeping that in sync with the database. Particularly if you're trying to build an asset management system, using a database to track and store all your binary and text data along with its metadata is going to be very attractive. Finally, if you're generating Web pages out of the database, you may have large blocks of text that do not fit into a VARCHAR, so you will want to take advantage of this feature and store that data as a BLOB.

Dealing with BLOBS from the database means dealing with I/O streams. Unlike the other SELECT calls we've made to the database up to this point, extracting a BLOB from the database returns a java.io.InputStream that must be read from, rather than the simple extraction of data that is done from a ResultSet object. If you're not familiar with this concept of reading and writing with streams, you'll need to review the java.io package. Suffice it to say that the mechanism is exactly like reading data from a file on disk or a network socket, except the source of the bytes is coming from within the database.

Even if you do not choose to store binary files in the database, the examples in this chapter can be retooled to read data from traditional disk-file systems by substituting the database calls for FileReader calls.

Load Balancing Between Objects

Keep in mind that by using BLOBS in your database schema you increase the amount of data going to and from the database via the network. Depending on the size of the data you're streaming around, you may encounter scalability issues. If you're pooling your connections, you'll probably want to create a special object with its own database connection to handle this kind of database access. Depending on your requirements, you may need multiple objects. However, this doesn't mean that you'll need to abandon your database API. In this chapter we'll cover how to integrate this kind of functionality into our existing UnitDB API.

Database Schema Design for BLOBS

Let's say we decide to include a picture for each item in our database where applicable. We add a table in the database to hold our images (this column could also hold movies, audio files, or compiled software programs if we wished) so there is a relationship to our UNIT table. See Figure 8–1.

The SQL to create this table looks like this:

```
create table image (
    id              number constraint pk_image primary key,
    unitid          number,
    format          number,
    image           long raw
)
/
alter table image add constraint fk_image foreign key (unitid)
    references unit (id)
/
alter table image add constraint fk_imageformat foreign key (format)
    references imageformat (id)
/
```

With Oracle, the LONG RAW datatype can contain data up to two gigabytes. We could have just added a LONG RAW column to the UNIT table, but this design allows us to have more than one picture or file per UNIT record if we decide we want that later.

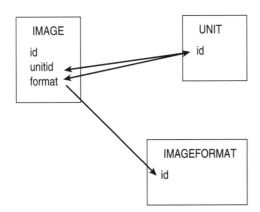

Figure 8–1: The relationship between the IMAGE and UNIT tables

Metadata

Note that this table contains a column for the actual binary data, as well as other columns to describe the binary data. These other columns are known as *metadata*. For instance, we can use the format column to tell what kind of data is in the IMAGE column before retrieving. (i.e., jpeg, gif, HTML, jar, Excel Spreadsheet, whatever). We could also add other columns that further describe the data. We could have dates to represent check-in and check-out times, or columns that track the backup tape this data is stored on, or whatever we require.

The important thing to remember is that when modifying the record we have to transfer the BLOB in a separate SQL call from the SQL that gets us the metadata. If we want to add a new image, we first have to insert a new record into the table in order to establish the relationship to the existing UNIT record while also defining the other attributes, such as file type, size, etc. Once that record has been successfully inserted, we then UPDATE the same record and set the BLOB column with our datastream from the client.

Adding BLOB Support in the API and Implementation

We'll add a couple of new methods to our API to handle this for us.

```
public synchronized int insertImageMetaData(int unitid, int formatid)
    throws RemoteException {
  int imageid = -1;
  String sql = new String();
  try {
      imageid = getNextSeq();
      sql = "insert into image (id, unitid, format) values ( " + imageid +
            "," + unitid + ", " + formatid + ")";
      Statement stmt = conn.createStatement();
      stmt.execute(sql);
      stmt.close();
  }
  catch (Exception e){
      RemoteException re = new RemoteException(sql + "\n" + e.getMessage());
      throw re;
  }

  return imageid;
}

public synchronized void updateImage(ByteArrayInputStream b,
                                     int size, int imageid)
      throws RemoteException {
  try {
      PreparedStatement pstmt = conn.prepareStatement(
```

```
                "update image set image = ? where id = ?" );
        pstmt.setBinaryStream (1, b, size);
        pstmt.setInt( 2,   imageid );

        pstmt.execute ();
        pstmt.close();
    }
    catch (SQLException se) {
        RemoteException re = new RemoteException(se.getMessage());
        throw re;
    }
}
```

Web-based Binary Content Delivery

Making Pretty Pictures in a Servlet—Scalability Issues

Yanking the images out of the database presents a bit of a scalability issue. Conceivably you could have fairly long single transactions as the data pours out of the database to the client. It makes sense to make a separate object with it's own database connection to handle this situation. That way people doing queries or modifying the database needn't be queued up waiting for the image to download.

We can accomplish this fairly easily by building a servlet that instantiates its own UnitDbImpl object. That will give it its own database connection. Since the servlet is by definition a server piece, we can still keep the number of database connections under control, as well as using HTTP instead of RMI to provide remote access to the database in this instance.

Multipart Form Encoding—Uploading Files

Let's say we want to let our users upload images from their Web browser. In order to accomplish this we're going to need to setup a Web form that uses multipart form encoding. Unfortunately, the servlet jdk 2.0 does not include an object that handles this for you by default. There are several examples of how to handle this type of form encoding available online and in books. Of course, I had to increase the number of these by one and include my own, specifically designed to make transferring the data to the database easier.

The basic notion of multipart form encoding is that each form element will be delimited by an ASCII delimiter string that is generated at runtime. Between the delimiters, there are key-value pairs describing the data that follows it. Here is an encoded form generated by POST from the ImageServlet form.

```
------------------10130224068002802421003853016
Content-Disposition: form-data; name="userfile"; filename="radio3.jpg"
Content-Type: image/jpeg
...
```

```
<data>
...
———————————-10130224068002802421003853016
Content-Disposition: form-data; name="unitid"

12
———————————-10130224068002802421003853016—
```

The MultiPartReader class will take this encoded form, and split the data into key-value pairs. You can then get a simple hashtable from it and retrieve your form objects by doing a simple hash.get(key) method call.

The way you use this class is in the doPost() method of a servlet, like this:

```
MultiPartReader mpr = new MultiPartReader(req);
Hashtable formhash = mpr.getFormData();
// get the form elements we need and expect from the form hashtable
Integer U = new Integer( (String) formhash.get("unitid") );
ByteArrayOutputStream b = (ByteArrayOutputStream) formhash.get("userfile");
String mime = (String) formhash.get("userfile" + "-mimetype");
```

Of particular interest for this exercise is that the formhash.get("userfile") will return an object of type ByteArrayOutputStream. Any uploaded file object will return as this object type. All other objects will be strings by default. This makes things easier for inserting into the database, as we'll see later.

Our Servlets

We actually need two separate servlets. One for adding or modifying the images in the database and another for image retrieval from the database.

A Servlet for Uploading Pictures

Now that we have all the tools to enable this functionality, let's get some pictures into the database. First, let's outline what we'll accomplish with this servlet:

- Provide an HTML form for uploading the image.

- Insert the image data into the database.

- Return the image data from the database so the user can validate the upload.

In order to enable this functionality, we need to have the servlet draw the form as a response to the HTTP GET request. We will require the database ID number for the unit that the picture refers to. In this way we will be able to call the form up by embedding a link wherever we need it, like this:

```
<a href="/servlets/UploadImageServlet?unitid=34>Upload Image</a>
```

If the servlet is called without an UNITID, we will complain and draw some pleasant HTML explaining the correct usage of the servlet.

When a UNITID is passed in, we will also look up some information on that UNIT so that the user can be sure what they are uploading against.

```
public void doGet (HttpServletRequest req, HttpServletResponse res)
    throws ServletException, IOException {
  ServletOutputStream out = res.getOutputStream();
  res.setContentType("text/html");

  String [] unitid = req.getParameterValues("unitid");
  if (unitid.length < 1) {
      out.println("you must provide the unitid to this servlet");
      out.close();
      return;
  } else {

      /*-----------------------------------------------------------*
       *   Grab the UnitInfo object for the passed in id. This will
       *   reassure the user that this is indeed the object they want
       *   to upload an image against.
       *-----------------------------------------------------------*/

      try {
          UnitInfo u = unitdb.getUnitInfo(
                          new Integer(unitid[0]).intValue());
          out.println("Updating image for: ");
          out.println(u.getName() + "<p>");
      }
      catch (RemoteException re) {
          log(re.getMessage());
      }

      /*-----------------------------------------------------------*
       *   build the actual form
       *-----------------------------------------------------------*/

      String form = "<form ENCTYPE=\"multipart/form-data\" " +
          "action=\"/servlets/ImageServlet\" method=\"POST\">" +
          "<INPUT TYPE=\"file\" size=40 NAME=\"userfile\"><br>" +
          "<input type=\"hidden\" name=\"unitid\" value=\"" +
          unitid[0] + "\"><br>" +
          "<input type=\"submit\" value=\"Engage\">" +
          "</form>";

      out.println(form);
  }

  out.close();
}
```

Next we need to handle the incoming form data, using the MultiPartReader object we introduced earlier.

```
public void doPost(HttpServletRequest req, HttpServletResponse res)
      throws ServletException, IOException {
   try {
        ServletOutputStream out = res.getOutputStream();
        res.setContentType("text/html");

        MultiPartReader mpr = new MultiPartReader(req);
        Hashtable formhash = mpr.getFormData();

        // get the form elements we need and expect from the form hashtable
        Integer U = new Integer( (String) formhash.get("unitid") );

        ByteArrayOutputStream b = (ByteArrayOutputStream) formhash.get("userfile");
        String mime = (String) formhash.get("userfile" + "-mimetype");


        int imageid = unitdb.insertImageMetaData(U.intValue(), 1);
        unitdb.updateImage( new ByteArrayInputStream(b.toByteArray()),
                                          b.size(), imageid);
        out.println("The following image was received:<p>");
        out.println("<img src=/servlets/GetImageServlet?imageid=" + imageid + ">");

   }
   catch (Exception e) {
        log(e.getMessage());
   }
}
```

Most of the nitty gritty of handling the binary stream input is handled by the MultiPartReader object. That's what makes this method call so short. Once we get the bytes from the MultiPartReader, we update the database using our updateImage call from our database API. Finally, we call the GetImageServlet to display the uploaded image back to the user so they can verify the transaction.

Hopefully by now you can see the benefit of all the time we spent building database APIs and utility objects. This servlet now has a very simple code base, and as such can be maintained by someone with only a cursory knowledge of Java programming. Modifications to the embedded HTML code could be easily made and found by Web designers and developers later.

A Servlet Displaying Pictures

The design of this servlet is a little different. It will probably get used more often and subsequently transfer a lot more data. Therefore we are going to want this servlet to have its own database connection and not use a broker. In order to also illustrate how to write a servlet that uses JDBC directly, we won't use the API for this servlet.

Like the database API, the servlet will keep a global connection object that gets instantiated with the init() method of the servlet, like so:

```
public class GetImageServlet extends HttpServlet {

    Connection conn;
    String url;

    public void init(ServletConfig config) throws ServletException {
        super.init(config);

        try {
        DriverManager.registerDriver (
            new oracle.jdbc.driver.OracleDriver ());

        url = "jdbc:oracle:thin:@localhost:1521:book";
        conn = DriverManager.getConnection (url, "stewartb",
                                            "stewartb");
        log("connected: " + conn);
        }
        catch (SQLException se) { log(se.getMessage()); }
}
```

Content MIME Types

The next trick in getting this to work is understanding how it's different from other servlets. First of all, you're not necessarily delivering ASCII text anymore. You're going to need to identify the data you're sending to the Web browser. In other servlets, we've done this with the command:

```
res.setContentType("text/html");
```

Now however, we are going to make it default to this:

```
res.setContentType("image/jpeg");
```

That will alert the browser that there is jpeg-encoded image data on the way. That's fine if all you want to see is the image, but how do we get it into a regular Web page?

The secret is to have your servlet be the value for the SRC variable in the IMG tag. Like this:

```
<img src="/servlets/GetImageServlet?unitid=34">
```

Now your other database-savvy servlets can simply embed this HTML tag in their output, substituting the actual UNITID that they want to display.

You could extend this design to have the servlet also read metadata from the database before streaming the binary content. In this way, you could have the servlet deliver MP3, MS Word documents, Gzipped Tar files, whatever.

Blasting Bits

Surprisingly, I've found the performance of this technique very good—although it can put a strain on an undersized database. However, if you're just delivering relatively small files, like jpeg images for Web pages, it should not be a problem at all.

All that's left to do is implement the doGet() method, pull the data out of the database, and write it out to the ServletOutputStream.

```
public synchronized void getImageForWeb(int imageid,
                                    ServletOutputStream out) {
    String sql = "select image from image where id = " + imageid;

    try {
        Statement stmt = conn.createStatement();
        ResultSet rs = stmt.executeQuery(sql);

        if ( rs.next()) {
          InputStream is;
          is = rs.getBinaryStream(1);
          int bytes_read = 0;
          byte [] buffer = new byte[4096];
          while ( (bytes_read = is.read(buffer, 0, buffer.length)) != -1) {
            out.write(buffer, 0, bytes_read);
          }
          is.close();
        }
        rs.close();
        stmt.close();
    }
    catch (Exception e){
        log(e.getMessage());
    }
}
```

It's important to note that this method is synchronized. That means that it can't be executed by more than one thread at a time. Otherwise you might start trying to pull data before you finished writing it out.

How It All Works Together

Our three servlets, UnitDbServlet, GetImageServlet, and ImageServlet all work together providing complementary functionality for our application. Figures 8–2 through 8–6 are screen shots showing the servlets in action. First, our user has used the UnitDbServlet to browse their way to the following part. They see that the image is outdated and decide to update it by following the link. The UnitDbServlet imbeds the database ID for the unit in the URL of the link, thus passing the information to the ImageServlet.

Next, the user gets an HTML form allowing them to select a new image from their local file system by clicking on the "Browse" button.

This in turn brings up the standard file system dialog for the user's OS, in this case Linux.

Finally, after selecting the desired file, the servlet displays the uploaded file back to the user as a verification of all things acting as expected.

Next time a user returns to that unit via the UnitDbServlet, they will see the new image.

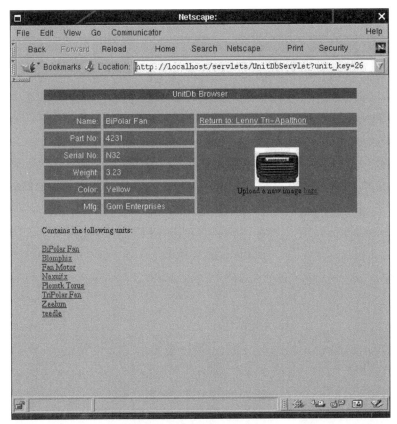

Figure 8–2: User clicks on the "Upload new image here" link

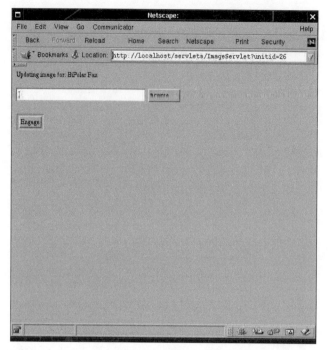

Figure 8–3: User gets the file upload form

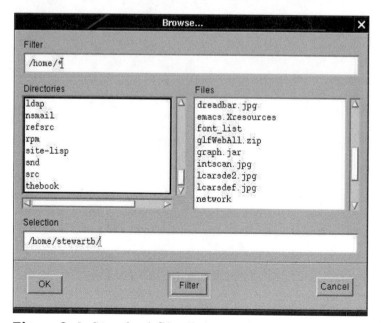

Figure 8–4: Standard file dialog as it appears in Linux

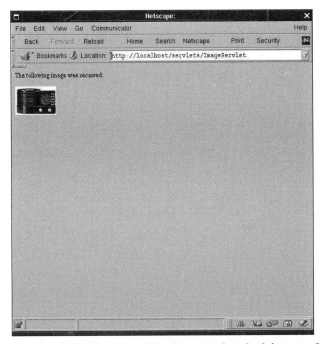

Figure 8–5: Servlet displays uploaded image back to user

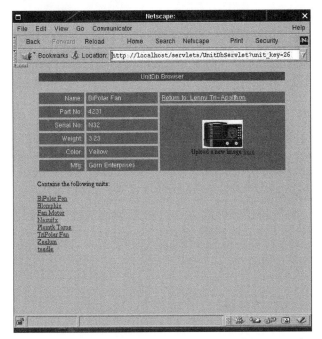

Figure 8–6: UnitDbServlet displaying new image

Code Listings

Listing 8–1: GetImageServlet.java

```java
/**
 * GetImageServlet.java
 *
 *
 * Created: Fri Dec  3 22:35:17 1999
 *
 * @author (c) 1999, 2000 Stewart Birnam
 * @version 1.0
 */

import java.io.*;
import java.sql.*;
import javax.servlet.*;
import javax.servlet.http.*;
import java.util.*;

public class GetImageServlet extends HttpServlet {

    Connection conn;
    String url;

    public void init(ServletConfig config) throws ServletException {
        // setup the db connectionyes
        super.init(config);

        try {
            //Class.forName ("oracle.jdbc.driver.OracleDriver");
            DriverManager.registerDriver (new oracle.jdbc.driver.OracleDriver ());

            // hard code the hostname and user/pass for now...
            url = "jdbc:oracle:thin:@localhost:1521:book";
            conn = DriverManager.getConnection (url, "stewartb", "stewartb");
            log("connected: " + conn);
        }
        //catch (ClassNotFoundException ce) { log(ce.getMessage()); }
        catch (SQLException se) { log(se.getMessage()); }
    }


    public void doGet (HttpServletRequest req, HttpServletResponse res)
            throws ServletException, IOException {
        ServletOutputStream out = res.getOutputStream();
        String [] is;
```

```
        String [] uid = req.getParameterValues("unitid");
        if (uid != null) {
            is = getImageId(new Integer(uid[0]).intValue());
            if (is.length < 1) {
              res.setContentType("text/html");
              out.println("no image on file. upload one " +
                  "<a href=/servlets/ImageServlet?unitid=" +
                  uid[0] + ">here</a>");
            }
        } else {
            is = req.getParameterValues("imageid");
        }
        if (is[0] != null) {
            // set content type and other response header fields first
            res.setContentType("image/jpeg");
            Integer I = new Integer(is[0]);
            if (I.intValue() > 0) {
                getImageForWeb(I.intValue(), out);
            }
        }

        out.close();
}

public synchronized void getImageForWeb(int imageid,
                                    ServletOutputStream out) {
    String sql = "select image from image where id = " + imageid;

    try {
        Statement stmt = conn.createStatement();
        ResultSet rs = stmt.executeQuery(sql);

        if ( rs.next()) {

            InputStream is;
            is = rs.getBinaryStream(1);
            byte [] buffer = new byte[4096];
            int i= 0;
            while ( ( i = is.read(buffer,0,buffer.length) ) != -1 ) {
                out.write(buffer,0,i);
            }
            is.close();
        }
        rs.close();
        stmt.close();
    }
    catch (Exception e){
         log(e.getMessage());
    }
}
```

```
public synchronized String [] getImageId(int unitid) {
    String sql = "select id from image where unitid = " + unitid;
    Vector imageid = new Vector();

    try {
        Statement stmt = conn.createStatement();
        ResultSet rs = stmt.executeQuery(sql);

        if ( rs.next()) {
            imageid.addElement(new String("" + rs.getInt(1)));
        }
        rs.close();
        stmt.close();
    }
    catch (Exception e){
        log(e.getMessage());
    }

    String [] s = new String[imageid.size()];
    for (int i=0; i<imageid.size(); i++) {
        s[i] = (String) imageid.elementAt(i);
    }
    return s;
}


public String getServletInfo() {
    return "ImageServlet spits out images by reading them from the " +
           "database as binary streams";
}

} // GetImageServlet
```

Listing 8–2: ImageServlet.java

```
import java.io.*;
import java.sql.*;
import javax.servlet.*;
import javax.servlet.http.*;
import java.util.*;
import java.rmi.*;

/**
 * ImageServlet.java
 *
 *
```

```
* Created: Fri Dec  3 22:35:17 1999
*
* @author (c) 1999, 2000 Stewart Birnam
* @version 1.0
*
*  This servlet handles inserting images into the database as BLOBs.
*  (Binary Large OBjects)
*  The doGet method returns the form used to upload the image.
*  The doPost method reads the MultiPart Form Encoding and inserts the
*  image into the database. It also returns the image uploaded for
*  confirmation.
*  This servlet also calls the UnitDbImpl object directly, thus holding
*  it's own database connection rather than using the remote object.
*  This serves as an example of using the API directly for
*  performance/load balancing reasons.
*/


public class ImageServlet extends HttpServlet {

    UnitDbImpl unitdb;

    public void init(ServletConfig config) throws ServletException {

        super.init(config);

        try {
            unitdb = new UnitDbImpl();
        }
        catch (RemoteException re) { log(re.getMessage()); }

    }

    /**
     * This method generates the form required for the doPost method. It
     * requires that the unitid be passed in.
     * The calling URL would be /servlets/ImageServlet?unitid=XXX.
     *
     * @param req a value of type 'HttpServletRequest'
     * @param res a value of type 'HttpServletResponse'
     * @exception ServletException if an error occurs
     * @exception IOException if an error occurs
     * @exception  if an error occurs       */
    public void doGet (HttpServletRequest req, HttpServletResponse res)
```

```
        throws ServletException, IOException {
    ServletOutputStream out = res.getOutputStream();
    res.setContentType("text/html");

    String [] unitid = req.getParameterValues("unitid");

    if (unitid.length < 1) {
        out.println("you must provide the unitid to this servlet");
        out.close();
        return;
    } else {

    /*------------------------------------------------------------*
     *  Grab the UnitInfo object for the passed in id. This will
     *  reassure the user that this is indeed the object they want
     *  to upload an image against.
     *------------------------------------------------------------*/

        try {
            UnitInfo u = unitdb.getUnitInfo(
                        new Integer(unitid[0]).intValue());
            out.println("Updating image for: ");
            out.println(u.getName() + "<p>");
        }
        catch (RemoteException re) {
            log(re.getMessage());
        }

    /*------------------------------------------------------------*
     *  build the actual form
     *------------------------------------------------------------*/

        String form = "<form ENCTYPE=\"multipart/form-data\" " +
          action=\"/servlets/ImageServlet\" method=\"POST\">" +
          "<INPUT TYPE=\"file\" size=40 NAME=\"userfile\"><br>" +
          "<input type=\"hidden\" name=\"unitid\" value=\"" +
          unitid[0] + "\"><br>" +
          "<input type=\"submit\" value=\"Engage\">" +
          "</form>";

        out.println(form);
    }


    out.close();
}

/**
 * doPost decodes the MultiPart form data and inserts a new Image
 *  into the database.it returns the uploaded image as selected out
```

```
 *   of the database to the browser as confirmation.
 * @param req a value of type 'HttpServletRequest'
 * @param res a value of type 'HttpServletResponse'
 * @exception ServletException if an error occurs
 * @exception IOException if an error occurs
 * @exception  if an error occurs
 */
public void doPost(HttpServletRequest req, HttpServletResponse res)
        throws ServletException, IOException {
    try {

        ServletOutputStream out = res.getOutputStream();
        res.setContentType("text/html");

        MultiPartReader mpr = new MultiPartReader(req);
        Hashtable formhash = mpr.getFormData();

        // get the form elements we need and expect from the form hashtable
        Integer U = new Integer( (String) formhash.get("unitid") );

        ByteArrayOutputStream b =
            (ByteArrayOutputStream) formhash.get("userfile");
        String mime = (String) formhash.get("userfile" + "-mimetype");

        if (b==null || U == null || mime==null) {
            out.println("cannot proceed without all necessary data<p>");
        }


        int imageid = unitdb.insertImageMetaData(U.intValue(), 1);
        unitdb.updateImage( new ByteArrayInputStream(b.toByteArray()),
                            b.size(), imageid);

        out.println("The following image was received:<p>");
        out.println("<img src=/servlets/GetImageServlet?imageid=" +
                    imageid + ">");

    }
    catch (Exception e) {
        log(e.getMessage());
    }
}


/**
 * a utility method for determining the actual form boundry.
 *
 * @param s a value of type 'String'
```

```
 * @return a value of type 'String'
 */
public String getBoundry(String s) {
    java.util.StringTokenizer st = new java.util.StringTokenizer(s, "=", false);
    st.nextToken();
    // the actual boundry has an extra "-" in front of this.... (sigh)
    String b = "-" + st.nextToken();
    // you'll also need the CR/LF that's tacked on the end
    // to properly split later. (ug)
    return  b + "\r\n";
}


public String getServletInfo() {
    return "ImageServlet spits out images by reading them from " +
            " the database as binary streams";
}
}
```

Listing 8–3: MultiPartReader.java

```
import java.io.*;
import java.util.*;
import javax.servlet.http.*;
import javax.servlet.*;
/**
 * MultiPartReader.java
 *
 *
 * Created: Tue Nov 30 22:30:13 1999
 *
 * @author (c)  1999, 2000 Stewart Birnam
 * @version 1.0
 */

public class MultiPartReader  {

    HttpServletRequest req;
    HttpServlet servlet;

    public MultiPartReader(HttpServletRequest r) {
        req = r;
    }
```

```java
public MultiPartReader(HttpServletRequest r, HttpServlet h) {
    req = r;
    servlet = h;
}


public Hashtable getFormData() throws IOException {
    String contenttype = req.getContentType();
    String boundry = getBoundry(contenttype);


    ServletInputStream is = req.getInputStream();

    byte [] formdata = new byte[req.getContentLength()];
    int offset = 0;
    int bytesread = 0;

    while (offset < req.getContentLength()) {
        bytesread = is.read(formdata, offset, req.getContentLength() );
        offset += bytesread;
    }

    String alldata = new String(formdata);

    // remove trailing weirdo — post-pended boundry
    alldata = alldata.substring(0, (alldata.length() - (boundry.length() + 4)));

    formdata = null;
    StringSplitter sp = new StringSplitter(alldata, boundry);
    Hashtable formhash = new Hashtable();
    String line, temp;

    // throw away the first null token
    sp.nextToken();

    while( (temp = sp.nextToken()) != null ) {
        BufferedReader br = new BufferedReader(new StringReader(temp));
        // line 1 contains the form element name, and filename if it's the file
        StringTokenizer stform = new StringTokenizer(br.readLine(), ";");
        stform.nextToken(); // throw first token away
        String value = new String();
        String keyname = new String();
        String filename = new String();
        String mimetype = new String();
        boolean isFile = false;
        ByteArrayOutputStream baos = new ByteArrayOutputStream();
```

```
while (stform.hasMoreTokens()) {
    String token = stform.nextToken();
    if (servlet != null) {
        servlet.log("token:" + token);
    }

    StringTokenizer keyval = new StringTokenizer(token, "=");
    String kn = keyval.nextToken();
    String v = keyval.nextToken();

    if (kn.equals(" name")) {
        if (v.startsWith("\"") && v.endsWith("\"")) {
            v = v.substring(1, v.length() -1);
        }
        keyname = v;
    }
    if (kn.equals(" filename") ){
        if (v.startsWith("\"") && v.endsWith("\"")) {
            v = v.substring(1, v.length() -1);
        }
        filename = v;
        isFile = true;
    } else {
        isFile = false;
    }

}

// line 2 - skip if not a file, contains content type
if (isFile) {
    String type = br.readLine();
    if ( type.indexOf("Content-Type") != -1) {
        StringSplitter ctype = new StringSplitter(type, ": ");
        ctype.nextToken(); // toss
        mimetype = ctype.nextToken();
        br.readLine(); // toss next line
    }
} else {
    br.readLine();
}
//line 3 - the actual value
if (isFile) {
    //no action...
} else {
    value = br.readLine();
}
```

```
        // more lines only happen for files
        if (isFile) {
            int p;
            baos = new ByteArrayOutputStream();
                while ( (p = br.read()) != -1) {
                    // write the data...
                    baos.write(p);
                }
            }

            if (isFile) {
                formhash.put(keyname, baos);
                formhash.put(keyname + "-mimetype", mimetype);
                formhash.put("filename", filename);
            } else {
                formhash.put(keyname, value);
            }
        }
        return formhash;
    }

    public String getBoundry(String s) {
        java.util.StringTokenizer st =
            new java.util.StringTokenizer(s, "=", false);
        st.nextToken();
        // the actual boundry has an extra "-" in front of this.... (sigh)
        String b = "-" + st.nextToken();
        // you'll also need the CR/LF that's tacked on the end
        // to properly split later. (ug)
        return  b + "\r\n";

    }


} // MultiPartReader
```

Listing 8–4: StringSplitter.java

```
/**
 * StringSplitter.java
 *
 *
 * Created: Sat Nov 27 09:18:09 1999
 *
 * @author (c) 1999, 2000 Stewart Birnam
 * @version 1.0
 *
 */
```

```java
public class StringSplitter {

    String str, delimiter;
    int start_position = 0;
    int start_delim = 0;

    /**
     * This class is much like StringTokenizer except it lets you use
     *  any length string to delimit with.
     *
     * @param s a value of type 'String', what you want to split up
     * @param d a value of type 'String', the delimiter to split by
     */
    public StringSplitter(String s, String d) {
        str = s;
        delimiter = d;
    }

    public String nextToken() {
        String s;
        start_delim = str.indexOf(delimiter, start_position);
        if (start_delim == -1 ) {
            if (start_position >= str.length()) {
                return null;
            } else {
                s = str.substring(start_position);
                start_position += s.length();
                return s;
            }
        }
        s = str.substring(start_position, start_delim);
        start_position = start_delim + delimiter.length();
        return s;
    }

    public static void main(String[] args) {
        String s = "foo--888999\r\nbar--888999\r\nboinx--888999" +
            "\r\nbinx--888999\r\n";
        StringSplitter sp = new StringSplitter(s, "--888999\r\n");
        String temp;
        while ( (temp = sp.nextToken() ) != null){
            System.out.println(temp);
        }
    }

} // StringSplitter
```

Chapter 9

Monitoring Tools and System Calls

- ▼ QUICK START
- ▼ TECHNOLOGY OVERVIEW
- ▼ USING RMI OBJECTS TO MONITOR USAGE AND SERVER STATUS

Quick Start

Here we give an example of a nondatabase use of RMI. It's a practical example of how to gather system information and send that info to a remote GUI. Essentially we implement xload with Java Swing and RMI instead of X/Motif. The result is a more customized monitoring tool that uses less network traffic and doesn't require the client to be running X. Great if you want your Win32 or Mac help-desk people to help monitor your systems.

Technology Overview

This chapter deals mostly with using Java technology to handle system and software administration issues. Most die-hards would probably not want to use Java technology to do what is traditionally regarded as system-level programming. However, you can use it to provide a high-level tool for accessing or integrating system components. Specifically, you can also use it to build command and control systems to monitor systems you design or systems you have integrated,

155

much in the same way Unix system administrators might use Perl or shell scripts to automate some of their tasks.

Be advised that making system calls accessible via RMI could open a security hole for you. You'll have to evaluate the wisdom of making features available to other machines via the network. In a closed, intranet environment, this would not be as great an issue as it would be in an Internet environment. Use common sense in enabling your features. If necessary, make use of the security features and APIs within Java to encrypt and authenticate your access.

For purposes of this chapter, we will not encrypt the traffic in any way. Be sure that you do not run the servers as root or any other privileged user on the system to prevent any potential security problems.

Using RMI Objects to Monitor Usage and Server Status

Now that we know so much about RMI, let's consider using what we've learned to help us monitor our servers remotely. In addition to wanting to know if our RMI server is up and functioning, we might want to know other things about the state of the system, like its current load, free disk space, available memory, etc. Most Unix system administrators would use a variety of tools to monitor the health of a system.

Some of these tools are graphical, requiring an X system to view. One example is xload, which draws a continually updating graph of the system load (Figure 9–1).

Most others are character based, like uptime, top, osview, w, and df to name but a few. Experienced Unix system administrators use these and other tools to gauge the health of a system. They often rely on a tool such as xload to watch overall system load, and then telnet into the system and start running one command or another if they see the system load go over some value known to be "too high."

While these methods are generally very efficient, they require an experienced administrator. Junior administrators and/or help-desk support staff generally have a harder time determining what is wrong with a system, and that bumps any problems immediately up to the senior people, making that first layer of support almost useless.

Figure 9–1: Xload

Java technology can help you build an "expert" monitoring tool that wraps up the knowledge of your best administrators and makes it accessible to your front-line support people whether or not they have X-capable workstations. This is accomplished by building a GUI in Java and using RMI to query the system remotely. Your client coalesces all the data and displays it in a organized fashion all at once, without the need for the person monitoring the system to make decisions as to which command to run first. In addition, you can have your "expert" monitoring tool make decisions based on the data it is receiving, and call up new displays, acquire additional data, make recommendations, or even notify other individuals via e-mail automatically.

Using Java to Make System Calls

Let's say that we want to build our own xload in Java. In order to acquire the data we need, we'll simply read the output of the uptime command and feed that into our graph.

CAUTION! Bear in mind that you are making a system call available over the network, perhaps in a very unsecure way. Always keep in mind the risks to your system by exposing these calls. As long as the information is not critical, and the system call that is made to get the info is not potentially dangerous, then it should be ok. Just make sure you carefully evaluate what you're doing and add the necessary safeguards where appropriate.

Wrapping RMI Around the System Calls

The Interface

Let's setup our interface first, outlining what people can expect to get from our object.

Listing 9–1: ShellCommand.java

```
public interface ShellCommand extends Remote {

    public String [] getLoad() throws RemoteException;

}
```

Ok, so that's not too much. But for now that'll do. Later on you could add other methods that return available disk space, users on the system, whatever you need. In our little, very specific world, we're just going to return an array of strings, corresponding to load values returned by the Unix uptime command.

The Implementation

Listing 9–2: ShellCommandImpl.java

```java
import java.rmi.*;
import java.rmi.server.*;
import java.io.*;
import java.util.*;
public class ShellCommandImpl extends UnicastRemoteObject implements ShellCommand{

    public ShellCommandImpl() throws RemoteException {

    }

    private synchronized String execCommand(String s) throws RemoteException{
        String z = "";
        String temp;
        try {
            Runtime r = Runtime.getRuntime();
            Process pr = r.exec(s);
            pr.waitFor();
            BufferedReader bis = new BufferedReader(
                new InputStreamReader( pr.getInputStream() ) );
            BufferedReader bes = new BufferedReader(
                new InputStreamReader(pr.getErrorStream()));

            while ( ( temp = bis.readLine() ) != null ) {
                z += temp;
            }
            while ( ( temp = bes.readLine() ) != null ) {
                z += temp;
            }

            bis.close();
            bes.close();
        }
        catch (Exception e) { e.printStackTrace(); }

        if ( z.length() < 1 ) {throw new RemoteException("ERROR: no data " +
                                                "received from system");}
        return z;
    }

    public synchronized String [] getLoad() throws RemoteException {
    // this method assumes the location of uptime and how it responds based
    // on Redhat Linux 6.1.
    // You may need to alter this code to run properly on another OS.

        String result = execCommand("/usr/bin/uptime");
        // parse out the three load values
        String delim = "load average:";
        int i = result.indexOf(delim);
        String  load = result.substring( (i + delim.length()) );
```

```
        StringTokenizer st = new StringTokenizer(load, ",");
        String [] lval = new String[st.countTokens()];
        int n=0;
        while (st.hasMoreTokens()) {
            lval[n] = st.nextToken().trim();
            n++;
        }


        return lval;
    }

    public static void main(String[] args) {
        try {
            ShellCommandImpl s = new ShellCommandImpl();
            String [] l = s.getLoad();
            for (int i=0; i< l.length; i++) {
                System.out.println(l[i]);
            }
            System.exit(0);

        }
        catch (Exception e) {
            e.printStackTrace();
        }
    }

}
```

NOTE: The execCommand method is private. This is due to the fact that you can use this method call to run *any* command on the system. By making it private we are allowing only this object to use this method so that we can carefully control its usage. This is a very important point, as I can tell the system to delete all my files or some other terrible thing just as easily as I can ask for the system load.

Ok, you've been warned—again.

The Server

Listing 9–3: MonitorServer.java

```
import java.util.*;
import java.rmi.*;
import java.rmi.registry.*;
import java.rmi.server.*;
public class MonitorServer {

    public MonitorServer() {

    }
```

```java
public static void main(String[] args) {
    // load a security manager if one already isn't in place...
    if (System.getSecurityManager() == null) {
        System.setSecurityManager(new RMISecurityManager());
    }

    // check for properties
    Properties p = System.getProperties();
    String rminame = p.getProperty("monitor.rminame");


    /*----------------------------------------*
     * one way or another, we spit out the properties we started
     * with to stdout.since our shell script redirects this to a
     * log file, we can easily check how the server was invoked
     * after the fact.
     *----------------------------------------*/

    p.save(System.out, "Starting Monitor Server with " +
                        "the following properties");

    try {
        ShellCommandImpl sc = new ShellCommandImpl();

        if (rminame != null) {
            Naming.rebind(rminame, sc);
        } else {
            Naming.rebind("MONITOR", sc);
        }
    }
    catch (java.net.MalformedURLException me) {
        me.printStackTrace();
        System.exit(1);
    }
    catch (RemoteException re) {
        re.printStackTrace();
        System.exit(1);
    }

    }

}
```

This sets up our object in the registry and now we can get to it remotely. Parameters can be passed in as with the servers we've already seen in previous chapters.

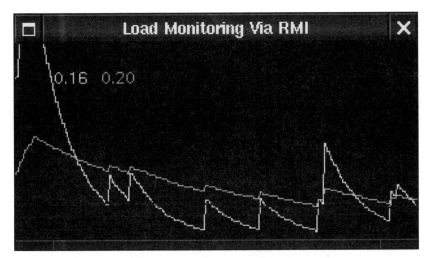

Figure 9–2: Our own notX-load via RMI

The Client

Graphics mumbo jumbo. You can handle the display of your data in any number of ways, and there are probably a lot more interesting ways to do it than what I'm going to show you, but this will get the job done. Quite simply, we're going to graph the load values we get, all three of them, into three different colored lines. As we collect more data, we'll slowly scroll the older data off as we add new data. When we're all done it will look like Figure 9–2.

We'll implement the runnable interface (since we're already extending JPanel) and use the thread to do our drawing to an offscreen buffer as well as get the latest results from our remote object. The mechanics of all this graphics code is the stuff of every tutorial on writing a Java Applet I've ever seen, and as such I won't review it again. Also, you could just as well simply print the results from the RMI call neatly to STDOUT, or animate a picture of a monkey climbing a pole. The point is that you can now monitor the system remotely from any platform without requiring an Xsession or remote login. Depending on your security arrangements, that may or may not be a good thing.

The code to make it happen looks like this:

Listing 9–4: MonitorPanel.java

```java
import javax.swing.*;
import java.awt.*;
import java.awt.event.*;
import java.rmi.*;
import java.util.*;
public class MonitorPanel extends JPanel implements Runnable{

    Thread thread;
    Image buff_image;
    Graphics buff_graphics;
    ShellCommand shellcommand;
    int width, height;
    Vector load1 = new Vector();
    Vector load2 = new Vector();
    Vector load3 = new Vector();
    FontMetrics fm;

    public MonitorPanel() {
        setBackground(Color.black);
        fm = getFontMetrics(getFont());
        try {
            shellcommand = (ShellCommand)
                Naming.lookup("rmi://localhost/MONITOR");
            start();
            width = getWidth();
            height = getHeight();
            }
            catch (Exception e) {
                e.printStackTrace();
            }
    }

    public void start() {
        thread = new Thread(this);
        thread.setPriority(Thread.MIN_PRIORITY);
        thread.setName("MonitorPanel");
        thread.start();
    }

    public void stop() {
        thread = null;
        notify();
    }

    public void run() {
        Thread me = Thread.currentThread();
        while (thread == me ) {
            try {
```

```
        if (width != getWidth() || height != getHeight()) {
            buff_image = (Image) createImage(getWidth(),
                                             getHeight());
        width = getWidth();
        height = getHeight();
    }

    while (load1.size() > width) {
        load1.removeElementAt(0);
        load2.removeElementAt(0);
        load3.removeElementAt(0);
    }

    if (buff_image != null) {

        buff_graphics = buff_image.getGraphics();
        buff_graphics.setColor(Color.black);
        buff_graphics.fillRect(0,0,width,height);
        buff_graphics.setColor(Color.yellow);

        String [] l = shellcommand.getLoad();

        load1.addElement(new Float(l[0]));
        load2.addElement(new Float(l[1]));
        load3.addElement(new Float(l[2]));

        buff_graphics.drawString(l[0], 30,30);
        buff_graphics.setColor(Color.orange);
        buff_graphics.drawString(l[1],
                        30 + fm.stringWidth(l[0]) + 10 ,30);
        buff_graphics.setColor(Color.blue);

        buff_graphics.drawString(l[2],
            30 + fm.stringWidth(l[0]) +
            10 + fm.stringWidth(l[1]) + 10,30);

        for (int n=0; n < load1.size(); n++) {
            buff_graphics.setColor(Color.yellow);

            Float f = (Float) load1.elementAt(n);
            int h = height - (int) (height * f.floatValue());
            Float f1;
            int h1;
            if (n >0) {
                f1 = (Float) load1.elementAt(n-1);
                h1 = height - (int) (height * f1.floatValue());

                buff_graphics.drawLine(n-1, h1, n, h);
            }

            f = (Float) load2.elementAt(n);
            h = height - (int) (height * f.floatValue());
            buff_graphics.setColor(Color.orange);
```

```
            if (n >0) {
                f1 = (Float) load2.elementAt(n-1);
                h1 = height - (int) (height * f1.floatValue());

                buff_graphics.drawLine(n-1, h1, n, h);
            }

            f = (Float) load3.elementAt(n);
            h = height - (int) (height * f.floatValue());
            buff_graphics.setColor(Color.blue);

            if (n >0) {
                f1 = (Float) load3.elementAt(n-1);
                h1 = height - (int) (height * f1.floatValue());

                buff_graphics.drawLine(n-1, h1, n, h);
            }
        }
        repaint();
    }
    thread.sleep(2000);
    }
    catch (Exception e) {
        e.printStackTrace();
    }
    }
}

public void paint(Graphics g) {
    if (buff_image != null) {
        g.drawImage(buff_image, 0, 0, this);
    }
    else {
        g.setColor(Color.black);
        g.fillRect(0,0,getWidth(),getHeight());
    }
}

public static void main(String[] args) {
    JFrame f = new JFrame("Load Monitoring Via RMI");
    MonitorPanel m = new MonitorPanel();
    f.getContentPane().add(m);
    f.setSize(200,200);
    f.setVisible(true);
    f.addWindowListener(new WindowAdapter () {
        public void windowClosing(WindowEvent e) {
            System.exit(0);
        }
    }
    );
}

}
```

Appendix A

Javadoc API Documentation for the Classes Used in This Book

DATABASE API

Interface UnitDb

All Known Implementing Classes:
> *UnitDbImpl*

---

public interface **UnitDb**
extends java.rmi.Remote

The UnitDB Interface. This is the template which we build the database API from. Notice that in this class we do not worry about the JDBC specific elements. Only the application specific elements are defined.

Version:
> 1.0

Author:
> (c)1999, 2000 Stewart Birnam

Method Summary

void	**deleteUnit**(int u)
java.util.Vector	**findColor**(java.lang.String s) findColor returns a Vector of UnitInfo objects that match the color name passed in.
java.util.Hashtable	**findUnit**(java.lang.String s) findUnit returns a hashtable of matches, key being a String of matching text and value being the database key for corresponding UnitInfo object.
java.util.Vector	**getChildUnits**(int u) getChildUnits is used to find all the units that are directly parented to the unit whose key is passed in.
java.util.Hashtable	**getColor**() getColor returns a hashtable with the key being the color name (String) and the value being the database key
java.util.Hashtable	**getMfg**() getMfg returns a hashtable containing a key/value pair with the key being a String (manufacturer name) and the value being an Integer (manufacturer database key).
UnitInfo	**getUnitInfo**(int u) getUnitInfo returns a complete UnitInfo object given that object's key.
int	**insertUnit**(UnitInfo u)
void	**updateUnit**(UnitInfo u)

Method Detail

insertUnit

```
public int insertUnit(UnitInfo u)
            throws java.rmi.RemoteException
```

updateUnit

```
public void updateUnit(UnitInfo u)
             throws java.rmi.RemoteException
```

deleteUnit

```
public void deleteUnit(int u)
             throws java.rmi.RemoteException
```

getChildUnits

```
public java.util.Vector getChildUnits(int u)
                          throws java.rmi.RemoteException
```

getChildUnits is used to find all the units that are directly parented to the unit whose key is passed in. This method is particularly useful for trees.
Parameters:
        u - a value of type 'int', the parent key.
Returns:
        a value of type 'Vector' containing UnitInfo objects
Throws:
        java.rmi.RemoteException - if an error occurs

getUnitInfo

```
public UnitInfo getUnitInfo(int u)
                  throws java.rmi.RemoteException
```

getUnitInfo returns a complete UnitInfo object given that object's key.
Parameters:
        u - a value of type 'int'
Returns:
        a value of type 'UnitInfo'
Throws:
        java.rmi.RemoteException - if an error occurs

getMfg

```
public java.util.Hashtable getMfg()
                        throws java.rmi.RemoteException
```

getMfg returns a hashtable containing a key/value pair with the key being a String (manufacturer name) and the value being an Integer (manufacturer database key).

Returns:
a value of type 'Hashtable'

Throws:
java.rmi.RemoteException - if an error occurs

getColor

```
public java.util.Hashtable getColor()
                        throws java.rmi.RemoteException
```

getColor returns a hashtable with the key being the color name (String) and the value being the database key

Parameters:
nil - a value of type "

Returns:
a value of type 'Hashtable'

Throws:
java.rmi.RemoteException - if an error occurs

findUnit

```
public java.util.Hashtable findUnit(java.lang.String s)
                        throws java.rmi.RemoteException
```

findUnit returns a hashtable of matches, key being a String of matching text and value being the database key for corresponding UnitInfo object.

Parameters:
s - a value of type 'String'

Returns:
a value of type 'Hashtable'

Throws:
java.rmi.RemoteException - if an error occurs

findColor

```
public java.util.Vector findColor(java.lang.String s)
                        throws java.rmi.RemoteException
```

findColor returns a Vector of UnitInfo objects that match the color name passed in.

Parameters:
s - a value of type 'String'

Returns:
a value of type 'Vector'

Throws:
java.rmi.RemoteException - if an error occurs

Class UnitDbImpl

```
java.lang.Object
  |
  +--java.rmi.server.RemoteObject
        |
        +--java.rmi.server.RemoteServer
              |
              +--java.rmi.server.UnicastRemoteObject
                    |
                    +--UnitDbImpl
```

public class **UnitDbImpl**
extends java.rmi.server.UnicastRemoteObject
implements *UnitDb*

UnitDbImpl.java Created: Wed Dec 29 22:58:15 1999

The implementation of the UnitDb interface.

Version:
     1.0
Author:
     (c) 1999, 2000 Stewart Birnam
See Also:
     Serialized Form

DATABASE API

Field Summary

private java.sql.Connection	**conn**
static int	**DB_DOWN**
java.text.SimpleDateFormat	**formatter**
private java.lang.String	**hostname**
private java.lang.String	**instance**
static int	**LSNR_DOWN**
private java.lang.String	**pass**
private java.lang.String	**url**
private java.lang.String	**user**

Fields inherited from class java.rmi.server.UnicastRemoteObject
csf, port, portFactoryParamTypes, portParamTypes, serialVersionUID, ssf

Fields inherited from class java.rmi.server.RemoteServer
log, logname, serialVersionUID

Fields inherited from class java.rmi.server.RemoteObject
ref, serialVersionUID

Constructor Summary

UnitDbImpl()   This constructor uses hard coded values.
UnitDbImpl(java.lang.String user, java.lang.String pass, java.lang.String hostname, java.lang.String instance)

Method Summary

void	**deleteUnit**(int i)
java.util.Vector	**findColor**(java.lang.String s) findColor returns a Vector of UnitInfo objects that match the color name passed in.
java.util.Hashtable	**findUnit**(java.lang.String s) findUnit returns a hashtable of matches, key being a String of matching text and value being the database key for corresponding UnitInfo object.
java.util.Vector	**getChildUnits**(int u) getChildUnits returns a vector of UnitNode objects.
java.util.Hashtable	**getColor**() getColor returns a hashtable with the key being the color name (String) and the value being the database key
java.util.Hashtable	**getImageType**()
java.util.Hashtable	**getMfg**() getMfg returns a hashtable containing a key/value pair with the key being a String (manufacturer name) and the value being an Integer (manufacturer database key).
int	**getNextSeq**() convience method to return the next value from an Oracle Sequence object.
java.io.InputStream	**getUnitImage**(int u)
UnitInfo	**getUnitInfo**(int u) getUnitInfo returns a complete UnitInfo object given that object's key.
int	**insertImageMetaData**(int unitid, int formatid)
int	**insertImageType**(java.lang.String s)
int	**insertUnit**(UnitInfo u)
static void	**main**(java.lang.String[] args)
void	**updateImage**(java.io.ByteArrayInputStream b, int size, int imageid)
void	**updateUnit**(UnitInfo u)

Methods inherited from class java.rmi.server.UnicastRemoteObject

clone, exportObject, exportObject, exportObject, exportObject, readObject, reexport, unexportObject

Methods inherited from class java.rmi.server.RemoteServer

getClientHost, getLog, setLog

Methods inherited from class java.rmi.server.RemoteObject

```
equals, getRef, hashCode, toString, toStub, writeObject
```

Methods inherited from class java.lang.Object

```
finalize, getClass, notify, notifyAll, registerNatives, wait, wait, wait
```

DATABASE API

Field Detail

conn

```
private java.sql.Connection conn
```

---

url

```
private java.lang.String url
```

---

user

```
private java.lang.String user
```

---

pass

```
private java.lang.String pass
```

---

instance

```
private java.lang.String instance
```

---

hostname

```
private java.lang.String hostname
```

DB_DOWN

```
public static final int DB_DOWN
```

LSNR_DOWN

```
public static final int LSNR_DOWN
```

formatter

```
public java.text.SimpleDateFormat formatter
```

Constructor Detail

UnitDbImpl

```
public UnitDbImpl()
        throws java.rmi.RemoteException
```

This constructor uses hard coded values.

Parameters:
nil - a value of type "

Throws:
java.rmi.RemoteException - if an error occurs
if - an error occurs

UnitDbImpl

```
public UnitDbImpl(java.lang.String user,
                  java.lang.String pass,
                  java.lang.String hostname,
                  java.lang.String instance)
        throws java.rmi.RemoteException
```

Method Detail

insertUnit

```
public int insertUnit(UnitInfo u)
        throws java.rmi.RemoteException
```

Specified by:
insertUnit in interface *UnitDb*

updateUnit

```
public void updateUnit(UnitInfo u)
        throws java.rmi.RemoteException
```

Specified by:
updateUnit in interface *UnitDb*

deleteUnit

```
public void deleteUnit(int i)
               throws java.rmi.RemoteException
```

> **Specified by:**
> *deleteUnit* in interface *UnitDb*

getChildUnits

```
public java.util.Vector getChildUnits(int u)
                      throws java.rmi.RemoteException
```

getChildUnits returns a vector of UnitNode objects. These are stripped-down versions of the UnitInfo object, containing just what is needed in a tree situation. This helps keep the potential transfer of large numbers of records fast.

> **Specified by:**
> *getChildUnits* in interface *UnitDb*
> **Parameters:**
> u - a value of type 'int'
> **Returns:**
> a value of type 'Vector'
> **Throws:**
> java.rmi.RemoteException - if an error occurs

getUnitInfo

```
public UnitInfo getUnitInfo(int u)
                  throws java.rmi.RemoteException
```

> **Description copied from interface:** *UnitDb*
> getUnitInfo returns a complete UnitInfo object given that object's key.

> **Specified by:**
> *getUnitInfo* in interface *UnitDb*
> **Tags copied from interface:** *UnitDb*
> **Parameters:**
> u - a value of type 'int'
> **Returns:**
> a value of type 'UnitInfo'
> **Throws:**
> java.rmi.RemoteException - if an error occurs

getMfg

```
public java.util.Hashtable getMfg()
                    throws java.rmi.RemoteException
```

Description copied from interface: *UnitDb*
getMfg returns a hashtable containing a key/value pair with the key being a String (manufacturer name) and the value being an Integer (manufacturer database key).

Specified by:
> *getMfg* in interface *UnitDb*

Tags copied from interface: *UnitDb*
Returns:
> a value of type 'Hashtable'

Throws:
> java.rmi.RemoteException - if an error occurs

getColor

```
public java.util.Hashtable getColor()
                            throws java.rmi.RemoteException
```

Description copied from interface: *UnitDb*
getColor returns a hashtable with the key being the color name (String) and the value being the database key

Specified by:
> *getColor* in interface *UnitDb*

Tags copied from interface: *UnitDb*
Parameters:
> nil - a value of type ''

Returns:
> a value of type 'Hashtable'

Throws:
> java.rmi.RemoteException - if an error occurs

findUnit

```
public java.util.Hashtable findUnit(java.lang.String s)
                            throws java.rmi.RemoteException
```

Description copied from interface: *UnitDb*
findUnit returns a hashtable of matches, key being a String of matching text and value being the database key for corresponding UnitInfo object.

Specified by:
> *findUnit* in interface *UnitDb*

Tags copied from interface: *UnitDb*
Parameters:
> s - a value of type 'String'

Returns:
> a value of type 'Hashtable'

Throws:
> java.rmi.RemoteException - if an error occurs

findColor

```
public java.util.Vector findColor(java.lang.String s)
                        throws java.rmi.RemoteException
```

Description copied from interface: *UnitDb*
findColor returns a Vector of UnitInfo objects that match the color name passed in.

Specified by:
    findColor in interface *UnitDb*
Tags copied from interface: *UnitDb*
Parameters:
    s - a value of type 'String'
Returns:
    a value of type 'Vector'
Throws:
    java.rmi.RemoteException - if an error occurs

getUnitImage

```
public java.io.InputStream getUnitImage(int u)
                            throws java.rmi.RemoteException
```

insertImageMetaData

```
public int insertImageMetaData(int unitid,
                        int formatid)
                    throws java.rmi.RemoteException
```

updateImage

```
public void updateImage(java.io.ByteArrayInputStream b,
                        int size,
                        int imageid)
                throws java.rmi.RemoteException
```

getImageType

```
public java.util.Hashtable getImageType()
                            throws java.rmi.RemoteException
```

insertImageType

```
public int insertImageType(java.lang.String s)
                    throws java.rmi.RemoteException
```

getNextSeq

```
public int getNextSeq()
            throws java.sql.SQLException
```

Convenience method to return the next value from an Oracle Sequence object. If using another database, you could define some unique id number generator here.

Returns:
a value of type 'int'
Throws:
java.sql.SQLException - if an error occurs

---

main

```
public static void main(java.lang.String[] args)
```

Class UnitDBServer

```
java.lang.Object
  |
  +--UnitDBServer
```

public class **UnitDBServer**
extends java.lang.Object

UnitDBServer.java

A simple RMI Server wrapper that makes use of properties. This class writes to STDOUT and STDERR, so that when debugging you can monitor the status from the command line, or redirect the output to log and error files as is common with Unix servers.

Created: Mon Oct 11 22:32:52 1999

Version:
   1.0
Author:
   (c) 1999, 2000 Stewart Birnam

Constructor Summary

```
UnitDBServer()
```

Method Summary

static void	**main**(java.lang.String[] args)

Methods inherited from class java.lang.Object

```
clone, equals, finalize, getClass, hashCode, notify, notifyAll, registerNatives,
toString, wait, wait, wait
```

Constructor Detail

UnitDBServer

`public UnitDBServer()`

Method Detail

main

`public static void main(java.lang.String[] args)`

Class UnitInfo

```
java.lang.Object
   |
   +--UnitInfo
```

public class **UnitInfo**
extends java.lang.Object
implements java.io.Serializable

UnitInfo.java Created: Thu Sep 23 23:08:27 1999

Version:
      1.0
Author:
      (c) 1999, 2000 Stewart Birnam
See Also:
      Serialized Form

Field Summary

(package private) java.util.Date	**cdate**
(package private) int	**colorid**
(package private) int	**id**
(package private) java.util.Date	**mdate**
(package private) int	**mfgid**
(package private) java.lang.String	**name**
(package private) int	**parentid**
(package private) java.lang.String	**parentname**
(package private) java.lang.String	**partno**
(package private) java.lang.String	**serialno**
(package private) float	**weight**

Constructor Summary

UnitInfo()
UnitInfo(int i, int p, java.lang.String n, java.lang.String pn, java.lang.String sn, float w, int c, int m, java.util.Date cd, java.util.Date md)   This constructor can be used to quickly populate a UnitInfo object.

Method Summary

java.util.Date	**getCdate**() Get the value of cdate.
int	**getColorid**() Get the UNIT colorid.
int	**getId**() Get the value of id, the primary database key for the UNIT table.
java.util.Date	**getMdate**() Get the value of mdate.
int	**getMfgid**() Get the UNIT mfgid.

DATABASE API

`java.lang.String`	`getName()` Get the unit name.
`int`	`getParentid()` Get the value of parentid, the key (ID) of the record in the database that this entity is a child of.
`java.lang.String`	`getParentname()` Get the value of parentname.
`java.lang.String`	`getPartno()` Get the UNIT partno.
`java.lang.String`	`getSerialno()` Get UNIT serialno.
`float`	`getWeight()` Get the UNIT weight.
`void`	`setCdate(java.util.Date v)` Set the value of cdate.
`void`	`setColorid(int v)` Set the UNIT colorid.
`void`	`setId(int v)` Set the value of id, the primary key for this entity.
`void`	`setMdate(java.util.Date v)` Set the value of mdate.
`void`	`setMfgid(int v)` Set the UNIT mfgid.
`void`	`setName(java.lang.String v)` Set the value of the UNIT name.
`void`	`setParentid(int v)` Set the value of parentid.
`void`	`setParentname(java.lang.String v)` Set the value of parentname.
`void`	`setPartno(java.lang.String v)` Set the UNIT partno.
`void`	`setSerialno(java.lang.String v)` Set the UNIT serialno.
`void`	`setWeight(float f)` Set the UNIT weight.
`java.lang.String`	`toString()` This is a method you can use to quickly view the object's contents .

Methods inherited from class java.lang.Object

`clone, equals, finalize, getClass, hashCode, notify, notifyAll, registerNatives, wait, wait, wait`

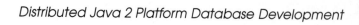
Field Detail

id

`int` **id**

---

parentid

`int` **parentid**

---

name

`java.lang.String` **name**

---

partno

`java.lang.String` **partno**

---

serialno

`java.lang.String` **serialno**

---

weight

`float` **weight**

---

colorid

`int` **colorid**

---

mfgid

`int` **mfgid**

---

cdate

`java.util.Date` **cdate**

---

mdate

```
java.util.Date mdate
```

parentname

```
java.lang.String parentname
```

Constructor Detail

UnitInfo

```
public UnitInfo()
```

UnitInfo

```
public UnitInfo(int i,
                int p,
                java.lang.String n,
                java.lang.String pn,
                java.lang.String sn,
                float w,
                int c,
                int m,
                java.util.Date cd,
                java.util.Date md)
```

> This constructor can be used to quickly populate a UnitInfo object. Quick only in the sense that you can build it all on one line. WARNING: using this constructor bypasses the validation logic, so use with care. This constructor can be useful when populating directly from the database, where the data is hopefully already validated.
> **Parameters:**
> > id - a value of type 'int'
> > parentid - a value of type 'int'
> > name - a value of type 'String'
> > partno - a value of type 'String'
> > serialno - a value of type 'String'
> > weight - a value of type 'float'
> > colorid - a value of type 'int'
> > mfgid - a value of type 'int'
> > creationDate - a value of type 'Date'
> > modificationDate - a value of type 'Date'

Method Detail

getId

```
public int getId()
```
> Get the value of id, the primary database key for the UNIT table.

Returns:
> Value of id.

---

setId

```
public void setId(int v)
```

> Set the value of id, the primary key for this entity.
> **Parameters:**
> > v - Value to assign to id.

---

getParentid

```
public int getParentid()
```

> Get the value of parentid, the key (ID) of the record in the database that this entity is a child of. If no parent is set, it will assume the root parent (0). If you wanted to make sure that the parentid was set by the application, you could make this object set it to -1 when instantiated and then test for that value in your application code. Even if you forget to test, Oracle will throw a SqlException from encountering an integrity constraint. As long as you haven't already inserted a record with -1 as the ID, that is!
> **Returns:**
> > Value of parentid.

---

setParentid

```
public void setParentid(int v)
```

> Set the value of parentid.
> **Parameters:**
> > v - Value to assign to parentid.

---

getName

```
public java.lang.String getName()
```

> Get the unit name.
> **Returns:**
> > UNIT name.

---

setName

```
public void setName(java.lang.String v)
```

> Set the value of the UNIT name.
> **Parameters:**
> > v - Value to assign to UNIT name.

getPartno

```
public java.lang.String getPartno()
```

> Get the UNIT partno.
> **Returns:**
> > Value of partno.

setPartno

```
public void setPartno(java.lang.String v)
```

> Set the UNIT partno.
> **Parameters:**
> > v - Value to assign to partno.

getSerialno

```
public java.lang.String getSerialno()
```

> Get UNIT serialno.
> **Returns:**
> > Value of serialno.

setSerialno

```
public void setSerialno(java.lang.String v)
```

> Set the UNIT serialno.
> **Parameters:**
> > v - Value to assign to serialno.

getWeight

```
public float getWeight()
```

> Get the UNIT weight.
> **Returns:**
> > Value of weight.

setWeight

```
public void setWeight(float f)
            throws BadWeightException
```

Set the UNIT weight.
Parameters:
    v - Value to assign to weight.

---

getColorid

```
public int getColorid()
```

Get the UNIT colorid.
Returns:
    Value of colorid.

---

setColorid

```
public void setColorid(int v)
```

Set the UNIT colorid.
Parameters:
    v - Value to assign to colorid.

---

getMfgid

```
public int getMfgid()
```

Get the UNIT mfgid.
Returns:
    Value of mfgid.

---

setMfgid

```
public void setMfgid(int v)
```

Set the UNIT mfgid.
Parameters:
    v - Value to assign to mfgid.

---

getCdate

```
public java.util.Date getCdate()
```

Get the value of cdate.
Returns:
    Value of cdate.

---

setCdate

```
public void setCdate(java.util.Date v)
```

> Set the value of cdate.
> **Parameters:**
>> v - Value to assign to cdate.

---

getMdate

```
public java.util.Date getMdate()
```

> Get the value of mdate.
> **Returns:**
>> Value of mdate.

---

setMdate

```
public void setMdate(java.util.Date v)
```

> Set the value of mdate.
> **Parameters:**
>> v - Value to assign to mdate.

---

getParentname

```
public java.lang.String getParentname()
```

> Get the value of parentname.
> **Returns:**
>> Value of parentname.

---

setParentname

```
public void setParentname(java.lang.String v)
```

> Set the value of parentname.
> **Parameters:**
>> v - Value to assign to parentname.

---

toString

```
public java.lang.String toString()
```

This is a method you can use to quickly view the object's contents . You may want to override this if you want to use this object in a GUI control or widget. In this form, you can just do:

System.out.println(unitinfo); ...and get a nice listing of the object values.

Overrides:

toString in class java.lang.Object

Parameters:

nil - a value of type"

Returns:

a value of type 'String'

Class IUDPanel

```
java.lang.Object
   |
   +--java.awt.Component
         |
         +--java.awt.Container
               |
               +--javax.swing.JComponent
                     |
                     +--javax.swing.JPanel
                           |
                           +--IUDPanel
```

public class **IUDPanel**
extends javax.swing.JPanel

IUDPanel.java Created: Tue Jul 27 16:01:13 1999

Version:
  1.0
Author:
  (c) 1999, 2000 Stewart Birnam
See Also:
  Serialized Form

Inner classes inherited from class javax.swing.JPanel
javax.swing.JPanel.AccessibleJPanel

Inner classes inherited from class javax.swing.JComponent
javax.swing.JComponent.AccessibleJComponent, javax.swing.JComponent.IntVector, javax.swing.JComponent.KeyboardBinding, javax.swing.JComponent.KeyboardState

Inner classes inherited from class java.awt.Component
java.awt.Component.AWTTreeLock

Field Summary

javax.swing.JButton	**cancelbutton**
javax.swing.JButton	**deletebutton**
javax.swing.JButton	**insertbutton**
javax.swing.JButton	**updatebutton**

Fields inherited from class javax.swing.JPanel

defaultLayout, uiClassID

Fields inherited from class javax.swing.JComponent

_bounds, accessibleContext, alignmentX, alignmentY, ANCESTOR_USING_BUFFER, ancestorNotifier, autoscroller, border, changeSupport, clientProperties, flags, HAS_FOCUS, IS_DOUBLE_BUFFERED, IS_OPAQUE, IS_PAINTING_TILE, IS_PRINTING, IS_PRINTING_ALL, KEYBOARD_BINDINGS_KEY, listenerList, maximumSize, minimumSize, NEXT_FOCUS, paintImmediatelyClip, paintingChild, preferredSize, readObjectCallbacks, REQUEST_FOCUS_DISABLED, tmpRect, TOOL_TIP_TEXT_KEY, ui, uiClassID, UNDEFINED_CONDITION, vetoableChangeSupport, WHEN_ANCESTOR_OF_FOCUSED_COMPONENT, WHEN_FOCUSED, WHEN_IN_FOCUSED_WINDOW

Fields inherited from class java.awt.Container

component, containerListener, containerSerializedDataVersion, dispatcher, layoutMgr, maxSize, ncomponents, serialVersionUID

Fields inherited from class java.awt.Component

actionListenerK, adjustmentListenerK, appContext, assert, background, BOTTOM_ALIGNMENT, CENTER_ALIGNMENT, changeSupport, componentListener, componentListenerK, componentOrientation, componentSerializedDataVersion, containerListenerK, cursor, dropTarget, enabled, eventMask, focusListener, focusListenerK, font, foreground, hasFocus, height, incRate, inputMethodListener, inputMethodListenerK, isInc, isPacked, itemListenerK, keyListener, keyListenerK, LEFT_ALIGNMENT, locale, LOCK, minSize, mouseListener, mouseListenerK, mouseMotionListener, mouseMotionListenerK, name, nameExplicitlySet, newEventsOnly, ownedWindowK, parent, peer, peerFont, popups, prefSize, RIGHT_ALIGNMENT, serialVersionUID, textListenerK, TOP_ALIGNMENT, valid, visible, width, windowListenerK, x, y

Constructor Summary

IUDPanel(int orientation)
   The IUDPanel (Insert-Update-Delete Panel) is a utility object for setting up the common gui components of a database entry GUI.

Method Summary

static void	**main**(java.lang.String[] args)

Methods inherited from class javax.swing.JPanel

getAccessibleContext, getUIClassID, paramString, updateUI, writeObject

---

Methods inherited from class javax.swing.JComponent

_paintImmediately, addAncestorListener, addNotify, addPropertyChangeListener,
addPropertyChangeListener, addVetoableChangeListener, adjustPaintFlags, alwaysOnTop,
bindingForKeyStroke, checkIfChildObscuredBySibling, computeVisibleRect, computeVisibleRect,
contains, createToolTip, enableSerialization, firePropertyChange, firePropertyChange,
firePropertyChange, firePropertyChange, firePropertyChange, firePropertyChange,
firePropertyChange, firePropertyChange, firePropertyChange, fireVetoableChange,
getActionForKeyStroke, getAlignmentX, getAlignmentY, getAutoscrolls, getBorder, getBounds,
getClientProperties, getClientProperty, getComponentGraphics, getConditionForKeyStroke,
getDebugGraphicsOptions, getFlag, getGraphics, getHeight, getInsets, getInsets,
getLocation, getMaximumSize, getMinimumSize, getNextFocusableComponent, getPreferredSize,
getRegisteredKeyStrokes, getRootPane, getSize, getToolTipLocation, getToolTipText,
getToolTipText, getTopLevelAncestor, getVisibleRect, getWidth, getX, getY, grabFocus,
hasFocus, isDoubleBuffered, isFocusCycleRoot, isFocusTraversable, isLightweightComponent,
isManagingFocus, isOpaque, isOptimizedDrawingEnabled, isPaintingTile,
isRequestFocusEnabled, isValidateRoot, keyboardBindings, paint, paintBorder, paintChildren,
paintComponent, paintImmediately, paintImmediately, paintWithBuffer, print, printAll,
processComponentKeyEvent, processFocusEvent, processKeyBinding, processKeyBindings,
processKeyBindingsForAllComponents, processKeyEvent, processMouseMotionEvent,
putClientProperty, readObject, rectangleIsObscured, rectangleIsObscuredBySibling,
registerKeyboardAction, registerKeyboardAction, registerWithKeyboardManager,
removeAncestorListener, removeNotify, removePropertyChangeListener,
removePropertyChangeListener, removeVetoableChangeListener, repaint, repaint,
requestDefaultFocus, requestFocus, resetKeyboardActions, reshape, revalidate,
scrollRectToVisible, setAlignmentX, setAlignmentY, setAutoscrolls, setBackground,
setBorder, setDebugGraphicsOptions, setDoubleBuffered, setEnabled, setFlag, setFont,
setForeground, setMaximumSize, setMinimumSize, setNextFocusableComponent, setOpaque,
setPaintingChild, setPreferredSize, setRequestFocusEnabled, setToolTipText, setUI,
setVisible, shouldDebugGraphics, superProcessMouseMotionEvent, unregisterKeyboardAction,
unregisterWithKeyboardManager, update

Methods inherited from class java.awt.Container

add, add, add, add, add, addContainerListener, addImpl, applyOrientation, countComponents,
deliverEvent, dispatchEventImpl, dispatchEventToSelf, doLayout, eventEnabled,
findComponentAt, findComponentAt, getComponent, getComponentAt, getComponentAt,
getComponentCount, getComponents_NoClientCode, getComponents, getCursorTarget, getLayout,
getMouseEventTarget, getWindow, initIDs, insets, invalidate, invalidateTree, isAncestorOf,
layout, lightweightPrint, list, list, locate, minimumSize, nextFocus, paintComponents,
postProcessKeyEvent, postsOldMouseEvents, preferredSize, preProcessKeyEvent,
printComponents, printHeavyweightComponents, printOneComponent, processContainerEvent,
processEvent, proxyEnableEvents, proxyRequestFocus, remove, remove, removeAll,
removeContainerListener, setCursor, setFocusOwner, setLayout, transferFocus, updateCursor,
validate, validateTree

Methods inherited from class java.awt.Component

action, add, addComponentListener, addFocusListener, addInputMethodListener, addKeyListener, addMouseListener, addMouseMotionListener, areInputMethodsEnabled, bounds, checkImage, checkImage, coalesceEvents, constructComponentName, contains, createImage, createImage, disable, disableEvents, dispatchEvent, enable, enable, enableEvents, enableInputMethods, getBackground, getBounds, getColorModel, getComponentOrientation, getCursor, getDropTarget, getFont_NoClientCode, getFont, getFontMetrics, getForeground, getInputContext, getInputMethodRequests, getIntrinsicCursor, getLocale, getLocation, getLocationOnScreen, getName, getNativeContainer, getParent_NoClientCode, getParent, getPeer, getSize, getToolkit, getToolkitImpl, getTreeLock, getWindowForObject, gotFocus, handleEvent, hide, imageUpdate, inside, isDisplayable, isEnabled, isEnabledImpl, isLightweight, isShowing, isValid, isVisible, keyDown, keyUp, list, list, list, location, lostFocus, mouseDown, mouseDrag, mouseEnter, mouseExit, mouseMove, mouseUp, move, nextFocus, paintAll, postEvent, prepareImage, prepareImage, processComponentEvent, processInputMethodEvent, processMouseEvent, remove, removeComponentListener, removeFocusListener, removeInputMethodListener, removeKeyListener, removeMouseListener, removeMouseMotionListener, repaint, repaint, repaint, resize, resize, setBounds, setBounds, setComponentOrientation, setDropTarget, setLocale, setLocation, setLocation, setName, setSize, setSize, show, show, size, toString, transferFocus

---

Methods inherited from class java.lang.Object

clone, equals, finalize, getClass, hashCode, notify, notifyAll, registerNatives, wait, wait, wait

Field Detail

insertbutton

public javax.swing.JButton **insertbutton**

---

updatebutton

public javax.swing.JButton **updatebutton**

---

deletebutton

public javax.swing.JButton **deletebutton**

---

cancelbutton

public javax.swing.JButton **cancelbutton**

Constructor Detail

IUDPanel

`public IUDPanel (int orientation)`

The IUDPanel (Insert-Update-Delete Panel) is a utility object for setting up the common gui components of a database entry GUI. The panel uses BoxLayout for presentation, so you can pass in either BoxLayout.X_AXIS or BoxLayout.Y_AXIS depending on your GUI's presentation.

The buttons are all public so that you can easily add listeners to them later.

Parameters:
>   `orientation` - a value of type 'int'

Method Detail

main

`public static void main(java.lang.String[] args)`

Class UnitDbClient

```
java.lang.Object
   |
   +--java.awt.Component
        |
        +--java.awt.Container
             |
             +--javax.swing.JComponent
                  |
                  +--javax.swing.JPanel
                       |
                       +--UnitDbClient
```

public class **UnitDbClient**
extends javax.swing.JPanel

UnitDbClient.java Created: Mon Oct 11 23:39:01 1999

This is the Swing database client that uses RMI to chat with the database via our UnitDb interface.

Version:
>   1.0
Author:
>   (c) 1999, 2000 Stewart Birnam
See Also:
>   *Serialized Form*

Inner Class Summary

class	`UnitDbClient.IUDListener`
(package private) class	`UnitDbClient.QueryListener`
(package private) class	`UnitDbClient.RadioListener`
(package private) class	`UnitDbClient.ResultListener`
class	`UnitDbClient.UnitTreeListener`

Inner classes inherited from class javax.swing.JPanel
`javax.swing.JPanel.AccessibleJPanel`

Inner classes inherited from class javax.swing.JComponent
`javax.swing.JComponent.AccessibleJComponent, javax.swing.JComponent.IntVector,` `javax.swing.JComponent.KeyboardBinding, javax.swing.JComponent.KeyboardState`

Inner classes inherited from class java.awt.Component
`java.awt.Component.AWTTreeLock`

Field Summary

(package private) javax.swing.JPanel	`cardpanel`
(package private) javax.swing.JComboBox	`colorcombo`
(package private) java.util.Hashtable	`colorhash`
(package private) java.util.Hashtable	`coloridhash`
(package private) javax.swing.DefaultComboBoxModel	`colormodel`
(package private) javax.swing.tree.DefaultMutableTreeNode	`current_node`
(package private) UnitInfo	`current_unit`
(package private) javax.swing.JComboBox	`mfgcombo`
(package private) java.util.Hashtable	`mfghash`
(package private) java.util.Hashtable	`mfgidhash`
(package private) javax.swing.DefaultComboBoxModel	`mfgmodel`
(package private) javax.swing.JTextField	`namefield`
(package private) javax.swing.JTextField	`partnofield`
(package private) javax.swing.JTextField	`queryfield`
(package private) java.util.Hashtable	`queryhash`

(package private) javax.swing.DefaultListModel	**querylist**
(package private) javax.swing.JList	**resultlist**
(package private) java.lang.String	**RMIHOST**
(package private) java.lang.String	**RMINAME**
(package private) javax.swing.JTextField	**serialnofield**
(package private) UnitTreeBrowser	**treepanel**
(package private) UnitDb	**unitdb**
(package private) javax.swing.JTextField	**weightfield**

Fields inherited from class javax.swing.JPanel

defaultLayout, uiClassID

Fields inherited from class javax.swing.JComponent

_bounds, accessibleContext, alignmentX, alignmentY, ANCESTOR_USING_BUFFER,
ancestorNotifier, autoscroller, border, changeSupport, clientProperties, flags, HAS_FOCUS,
IS_DOUBLE_BUFFERED, IS_OPAQUE, IS_PAINTING_TILE, IS_PRINTING, IS_PRINTING_ALL,
KEYBOARD_BINDINGS_KEY, listenerList, maximumSize, minimumSize, NEXT_FOCUS,
paintImmediatelyClip, paintingChild, preferredSize, readObjectCallbacks,
REQUEST_FOCUS_DISABLED, tmpRect, TOOL_TIP_TEXT_KEY, ui, uiClassID, UNDEFINED_CONDITION,
vetoableChangeSupport, WHEN_ANCESTOR_OF_FOCUSED_COMPONENT, WHEN_FOCUSED,
WHEN_IN_FOCUSED_WINDOW

Fields inherited from class java.awt.Container

component, containerListener, containerSerializedDataVersion, dispatcher, layoutMgr,
maxSize, ncomponents, serialVersionUID

Fields inherited from class java.awt.Component

actionListenerK, adjustmentListenerK, appContext, assert, background, BOTTOM_ALIGNMENT,
CENTER_ALIGNMENT, changeSupport, componentListener, componentListenerK,
componentOrientation, componentSerializedDataVersion, containerListenerK, cursor,
dropTarget, enabled, eventMask, focusListener, focusListenerK, font, foreground, hasFocus,
height, incRate, inputMethodListener, inputMethodListenerK, isInc, isPacked, itemListenerK,
keyListener, keyListenerK, LEFT_ALIGNMENT, locale, LOCK, minSize, mouseListener,
mouseListenerK, mouseMotionListener, mouseMotionListenerK, name, nameExplicitlySet,
newEventsOnly, ownedWindowK, parent, peer, peerFont, popups, prefSize, RIGHT_ALIGNMENT,
serialVersionUID, textListenerK, TOP_ALIGNMENT, valid, visible, width,
windowListenerK, x, y

Constructor Summary

| **UnitDbClient**() |
| Default Constructor. |

| **UnitDbClient**(java.lang.String n, java.lang.String h) |
| This constructor lets you specify the RMI object name in the registry as well as the hostname. |

| **UnitDbClient**(UnitDb u) |
| This constructor lets you pass in the remote object by reference. |

Method Summary

void	**displayError**(java.lang.Exception e)
UnitInfo	**getUnitInfo**() getUnitInfo returns a UnitInfo object for passing to the UnitDb insert, and update methods.
void	**init**()
(package private) void	**initfieldpanel**(javax.swing.JPanel p)
(package private) void	**initQueryPanel**(javax.swing.JPanel p)
void	**initRMI**(java.lang.String host, java.lang.String rname)
(package private) void	**initSearchOptionPanel**(javax.swing.JPanel p)
static void	**main**(java.lang.String[] args)
void	**setUnitInfo**(UnitInfo u)

Methods inherited from class javax.swing.JPanel

getAccessibleContext, getUIClassID, paramString, updateUI, writeObject

SWING RMI CLIENT

Methods inherited from class javax.swing.JComponent

_paintImmediately, addAncestorListener, addNotify, addPropertyChangeListener,
addPropertyChangeListener, addVetoableChangeListener, adjustPaintFlags, alwaysOnTop,
bindingForKeyStroke, checkIfChildObscuredBySibling, computeVisibleRect, computeVisibleRect,
contains, createToolTip, enableSerialization, firePropertyChange, firePropertyChange,
firePropertyChange, firePropertyChange, firePropertyChange, firePropertyChange,
firePropertyChange, firePropertyChange, firePropertyChange, fireVetoableChange,
getActionForKeyStroke, getAlignmentX, getAlignmentY, getAutoscrolls, getBorder, getBounds,
getClientProperties, getClientProperty, getComponentGraphics, getConditionForKeyStroke,
getDebugGraphicsOptions, getFlag, getGraphics, getHeight, getInsets, getInsets,
getLocation, getMaximumSize, getMinimumSize, getNextFocusableComponent, getPreferredSize,
getRegisteredKeyStrokes, getRootPane, getSize, getToolTipLocation, getToolTipText,
getToolTipText, getTopLevelAncestor, getVisibleRect, getWidth, getX, getY, grabFocus,
hasFocus, isDoubleBuffered, isFocusCycleRoot, isFocusTraversable, isLightweightComponent,
isManagingFocus, isOpaque, isOptimizedDrawingEnabled, isPaintingTile,
isRequestFocusEnabled, isValidateRoot, keyboardBindings, paint, paintBorder, paintChildren,
paintComponent, paintImmediately, paintImmediately, paintWithBuffer, print, printAll,
processComponentKeyEvent, processFocusEvent, processKeyBinding, processKeyBindings,
processKeyBindingsForAllComponents, processKeyEvent, processMouseMotionEvent,
putClientProperty, readObject, rectangleIsObscured, rectangleIsObscuredBySibling,
registerKeyboardAction, registerKeyboardAction, registerWithKeyboardManager,
removeAncestorListener, removeNotify, removePropertyChangeListener,
removePropertyChangeListener, removeVetoableChangeListener, repaint, repaint,
requestDefaultFocus, requestFocus, resetKeyboardActions, reshape, revalidate,
scrollRectToVisible, setAlignmentX, setAlignmentY, setAutoscrolls, setBackground,
setBorder, setDebugGraphicsOptions, setDoubleBuffered, setEnabled, setFlag, setFont,
setForeground, setMaximumSize, setMinimumSize, setNextFocusableComponent, setOpaque,
setPaintingChild, setPreferredSize, setRequestFocusEnabled, setToolTipText, setUI,
setVisible, shouldDebugGraphics, superProcessMouseMotionEvent, unregisterKeyboardAction,
unregisterWithKeyboardManager, update

Methods inherited from class java.awt.Container

add, add, add, add, add, addContainerListener, addImpl, applyOrientation, countComponents,
deliverEvent, dispatchEventImpl, dispatchEventToSelf, doLayout, eventEnabled,
findComponentAt, findComponentAt, getComponent, getComponentAt, getComponentAt,
getComponentCount, getComponents_NoClientCode, getComponents, getCursorTarget, getLayout,
getMouseEventTarget, getWindow, initIDs, insets, invalidate, invalidateTree, isAncestorOf,
layout, lightweightPrint, list, list, locate, minimumSize, nextFocus, paintComponents,
postProcessKeyEvent, postsOldMouseEvents, preferredSize, preProcessKeyEvent,
printComponents, printHeavyweightComponents, printOneComponent, processContainerEvent,
processEvent, proxyEnableEvents, proxyRequestFocus, remove, remove, removeAll,
removeContainerListener, setCursor, setFocusOwner, setLayout, transferFocus, updateCursor,
validate, validateTree

Methods inherited from class java.awt.Component

action, add, addComponentListener, addFocusListener, addInputMethodListener, addKeyListener, addMouseListener, addMouseMotionListener, areInputMethodsEnabled, bounds, checkImage, checkImage, coalesceEvents, constructComponentName, contains, createImage, createImage, disable, disableEvents, dispatchEvent, enable, enable, enableEvents, enableInputMethods, getBackground, getBounds, getColorModel, getComponentOrientation, getCursor, getDropTarget, getFont_NoClientCode, getFont, getFontMetrics, getForeground, getInputContext, getInputMethodRequests, getIntrinsicCursor, getLocale, getLocation, getLocationOnScreen, getName, getNativeContainer, getParent_NoClientCode, getParent, getPeer, getSize, getToolkit, getToolkitImpl, getTreeLock, getWindowForObject, gotFocus, handleEvent, hide, imageUpdate, inside, isDisplayable, isEnabled, isEnabledImpl, isLightweight, isShowing, isValid, isVisible, keyDown, keyUp, list, list, list, location, lostFocus, mouseDown, mouseDrag, mouseEnter, mouseExit, mouseMove, mouseUp, move, nextFocus, paintAll, postEvent, prepareImage, prepareImage, processComponentEvent, processInputMethodEvent, processMouseEvent, remove, removeComponentListener, removeFocusListener, removeInputMethodListener, removeKeyListener, removeMouseListener, removeMouseMotionListener, repaint, repaint, repaint, resize, resize, setBounds, setBounds, setComponentOrientation, setDropTarget, setLocale, setLocation, setLocation, setName, setSize, setSize, show, show, size, toString, transferFocus

---

Methods inherited from class java.lang.Object

clone, equals, finalize, getClass, hashCode, notify, notifyAll, registerNatives, wait, wait, wait

Field Detail

RMINAME

java.lang.String **RMINAME**

RMIHOST

java.lang.String **RMIHOST**

---

unitdb

UnitDb **unitdb**

---

current_unit

UnitInfo **current_unit**

---

cardpanel

`javax.swing.JPanel` **`cardpanel`**

---

colorcombo

`javax.swing.JComboBox` **`colorcombo`**

---

mfgcombo

`javax.swing.JComboBox` **`mfgcombo`**

---

namefield

`javax.swing.JTextField` **`namefield`**

---

partnofield

`javax.swing.JTextField` **`partnofield`**

---

serialnofield

`javax.swing.JTextField` **`serialnofield`**

---

weightfield

`javax.swing.JTextField` **`weightfield`**

---

queryfield

`javax.swing.JTextField` **`queryfield`**

---

treepanel

`UnitTreeBrowser` **`treepanel`**

---

current_node

`javax.swing.tree.DefaultMutableTreeNode` **`current_node`**

resultlist

`javax.swing.JList` **`resultlist`**

colorhash

`java.util.Hashtable` **`colorhash`**

mfghash

`java.util.Hashtable` **`mfghash`**

coloridhash

`java.util.Hashtable` **`coloridhash`**

mfgidhash

`java.util.Hashtable` **`mfgidhash`**

queryhash

`java.util.Hashtable` **`queryhash`**

colormodel

`javax.swing.DefaultComboBoxModel` **`colormodel`**

mfgmodel

`javax.swing.DefaultComboBoxModel` **`mfgmodel`**

querylist

`javax.swing.DefaultListModel` **`querylist`**

Constructor Detail

UnitDbClient

```
public UnitDbClient()
```

> Default Constructor. Uses hardcoded values.

UnitDbClient

```
public UnitDbClient(java.lang.String n,
                    java.lang.String h)
```

> This constructor lets you specify the RMI object name in the registry as well as the hostname.
> **Parameters:**
> > RMINAME, - the name of the remote object in the registry - a value of type 'String'
> > HOSTNAME, - the hostname of the RMI server - a value of type 'String'

UnitDbClient

```
public UnitDbClient(UnitDb u)
```

> This constructor lets you pass in the remote object by reference.
> **Parameters:**
> > u - a value of type 'UnitDb'

Method Detail

init

```
public void init()
```

---

initRMI

```
public void initRMI(java.lang.String host,
                    java.lang.String rname)
```

---

initQueryPanel

```
void initQueryPanel(javax.swing.JPanel p)
```

---

initSearchOptionPanel

```
void initSearchOptionPanel(javax.swing.JPanel p)
```

initfieldpanel

```
void initfieldpanel(javax.swing.JPanel p)
```

getUnitInfo

```
public UnitInfo getUnitInfo()
```

> getUnitInfo returns a UnitInfo object for passing to the UnitDb insert, and update methods. It builds the UnitInfo object by pulling values from the current state of the GUI. Additional validation could occur here to insure that everything is as it should be before passing the values to the database.
>
> **Returns:**
> > a value of type 'UnitInfo'

setUnitInfo

```
public void setUnitInfo(UnitInfo u)
```

displayError

```
public void displayError(java.lang.Exception e)
```

main

```
public static void main(java.lang.String[] args)
```

SWING RMI CLIENT

Class UnitNode

```
java.lang.Object
  |
  +--UnitNode
```

public class **UnitNode**
extends java.lang.Object
implements java.io.Serializable

UnitNode.java Created: Thu Sep 23 23:08:27 1999

Version:
  1.0
Author:
  (c) 1999, 2000 Stewart Birnam
See Also:
  Serialized Form

Field Summary

(package private) int	**id**
(package private) java.lang.String	**name**
(package private) int	**parentid**
(package private) java.lang.String	**parentname**

Constructor Summary

UnitNode()
UnitNode(int i, int j, java.lang.String s)

Method Summary

int	**getId**() Get the value of id.
java.lang.String	**getName**() Get the value of name.
int	**getParentid**() Get the value of parentid.
java.lang.String	**getParentname**() Get the value of parentname.
void	**setId**(int v) Set the value of id.
void	**setName**(java.lang.String v) Set the value of name.
void	**setParentid**(int v) Set the value of parentid.
void	**setParentname**(java.lang.String v) Set the value of parentname.
java.lang.String	**toString**()

Methods inherited from class java.lang.Object

clone, equals, finalize, getClass, hashCode, notify, notifyAll, registerNatives, wait, wait, wait

Field Detail

id

int **id**

---

parentid

int **parentid**

---

name

java.lang.String **name**

---

parentname

`java.lang.String parentname`

Constructor Detail

UnitNode

`public UnitNode()`

UnitNode

```
public UnitNode(int i,
                int j,
                java.lang.String s)
```

Method Detail

getId

`public int getId()`

> Get the value of id.
> **Returns:**
> > Value of id.

setId

`public void setId(int v)`

> Set the value of id.
> **Parameters:**
> > v - Value to assign to id.

getParentid

`public int getParentid()`

> Get the value of parentid.
> **Returns:**
> > Value of parentid.

setParentid

`public void setParentid(int v)`

> Set the value of parentid.
> **Parameters:**
> > v - Value to assign to parentid.

getName

```
public java.lang.String getName()
```

> Get the value of name.
> **Returns:**
> > Value of name.

setName

```
public void setName(java.lang.String v)
```

> Set the value of name.
> **Parameters:**
> > v - Value to assign to name.

getParentname

```
public java.lang.String getParentname()
```

> Get the value of parentname.
> **Returns:**
> > Value of parentname.

setParentname

```
public void setParentname(java.lang.String v)
```

> Set the value of parentname.
> **Parameters:**
> > v - Value to assign to parentname.

toString

```
public java.lang.String toString()
```

> **Overrides:**
> > toString in class java.lang.Object

SWING RMI CLIENT

Class UnitTreeBrowser

```
java.lang.Object
  |
  +--java.awt.Component
       |
       +--java.awt.Container
            |
            +--javax.swing.JComponent
                 |
                 +--javax.swing.JPanel
                      |
                      +--UnitTreeBrowser
```

public class **UnitTreeBrowser**
extends javax.swing.JPanel

UnitTreeBrowser.java Created: Wed Nov 3 20:31:33 1999

Version:
      1.0
Author:
      (c) 1999, 2000 Stewart Birnam
See Also:
      Serialized Form

Inner Class Summary

class	UnitTreeBrowser.DefaultUnitTreeListener

Inner classes inherited from class javax.swing.JPanel

javax.swing.JPanel.AccessibleJPanel

Inner classes inherited from class javax.swing.JComponent

javax.swing.JComponent.AccessibleJComponent, javax.swing.JComponent.IntVector,
javax.swing.JComponent.KeyboardBinding, javax.swing.JComponent.KeyboardState

Inner classes inherited from class java.awt.Component

java.awt.Component.AWTTreeLock

Field Summary

(package private) UnitNode	**LAST_NODE**
(package private) UnitNode	**TOP_NODE**
javax.swing.tree.DefaultMutableTreeNode	**TOP_TREE**
javax.swing.JTree	**tree**
(package private) javax.swing.JScrollPane	**treeview**
(package private) javax.swing.event.TreeSelectionListener	**TSL**
(package private) UnitDb	**unitdb**

Fields inherited from class javax.swing.JPanel

defaultLayout, uiClassID

Fields inherited from class javax.swing.JComponent

_bounds, accessibleContext, alignmentX, alignmentY, ANCESTOR_USING_BUFFER,
ancestorNotifier, autoscroller, border, changeSupport, clientProperties, flags, HAS_FOCUS,
IS_DOUBLE_BUFFERED, IS_OPAQUE, IS_PAINTING_TILE, IS_PRINTING, IS_PRINTING_ALL,
KEYBOARD_BINDINGS_KEY, listenerList, maximumSize, minimumSize, NEXT_FOCUS,
paintImmediatelyClip, paintingChild, preferredSize, readObjectCallbacks,
REQUEST_FOCUS_DISABLED, tmpRect, TOOL_TIP_TEXT_KEY, ui, uiClassID, UNDEFINED_CONDITION,
vetoableChangeSupport, WHEN_ANCESTOR_OF_FOCUSED_COMPONENT, WHEN_FOCUSED,
WHEN_IN_FOCUSED_WINDOW

Fields inherited from class java.awt.Container

component, containerListener, containerSerializedDataVersion, dispatcher, layoutMgr,
maxSize, ncomponents, serialVersionUID

Fields inherited from class java.awt.Component

actionListenerK, adjustmentListenerK, appContext, assert, background, BOTTOM_ALIGNMENT,
CENTER_ALIGNMENT, changeSupport, componentListener, componentListenerK,
componentOrientation, componentSerializedDataVersion, containerListenerK, cursor,
dropTarget, enabled, eventMask, focusListener, focusListenerK, font, foreground, hasFocus,
height, incRate, inputMethodListener, inputMethodListenerK, isInc, isPacked, itemListenerK,
keyListener, keyListenerK, LEFT_ALIGNMENT, locale, LOCK, minSize, mouseListener,
mouseListenerK, mouseMotionListener, mouseMotionListenerK, name, nameExplicitlySet,
newEventsOnly, ownedWindowK, parent, peer, peerFont, popups, prefSize, RIGHT_ALIGNMENT,
serialVersionUID, textListenerK, TOP_ALIGNMENT, valid, visible, width,
windowListenerK, x, y

Constructor Summary

UnitTreeBrowser(UnitDb u)

Method Summary

void	**addTreeListener**(javax.swing.event.TreeSelectionListener t)
void	**createNodes**(javax.swing.tree.DefaultMutableTreeNode top)
static void	**main**(java.lang.String[] args)

Methods inherited from class javax.swing.JPanel

getAccessibleContext, getUIClassID, paramString, updateUI, writeObject

Methods inherited from class javax.swing.JComponent

_paintImmediately, addAncestorListener, addNotify, addPropertyChangeListener, addPropertyChangeListener, addVetoableChangeListener, adjustPaintFlags, alwaysOnTop, bindingForKeyStroke, checkIfChildObscuredBySibling, computeVisibleRect, computeVisibleRect, contains, createToolTip, enableSerialization, firePropertyChange, firePropertyChange, firePropertyChange, firePropertyChange, firePropertyChange, firePropertyChange, firePropertyChange, firePropertyChange, firePropertyChange, fireVetoableChange, getActionForKeyStroke, getAlignmentX, getAlignmentY, getAutoscrolls, getBorder, getBounds, getClientProperties, getClientProperty, getComponentGraphics, getConditionForKeyStroke, getDebugGraphicsOptions, getFlag, getGraphics, getHeight, getInsets, getInsets, getLocation, getMaximumSize, getMinimumSize, getNextFocusableComponent, getPreferredSize, getRegisteredKeyStrokes, getRootPane, getSize, getToolTipLocation, getToolTipText, getToolTipText, getTopLevelAncestor, getVisibleRect, getWidth, getX, getY, grabFocus, hasFocus, isDoubleBuffered, isFocusCycleRoot, isFocusTraversable, isLightweightComponent, isManagingFocus, isOpaque, isOptimizedDrawingEnabled, isPaintingTile, isRequestFocusEnabled, isValidateRoot, keyboardBindings, paint, paintBorder, paintChildren, paintComponent, paintImmediately, paintImmediately, paintWithBuffer, print, printAll, processComponentKeyEvent, processFocusEvent, processKeyBinding, processKeyBindings, processKeyBindingsForAllComponents, processKeyEvent, processMouseMotionEvent, putClientProperty, readObject, rectangleIsObscured, rectangleIsObscuredBySibling, registerKeyboardAction, registerKeyboardAction, registerWithKeyboardManager, removeAncestorListener, removeNotify, removePropertyChangeListener, removePropertyChangeListener, removeVetoableChangeListener, repaint, repaint, requestDefaultFocus, requestFocus, resetKeyboardActions, reshape, revalidate, scrollRectToVisible, setAlignmentX, setAlignmentY, setAutoscrolls, setBackground, setBorder, setDebugGraphicsOptions, setDoubleBuffered, setEnabled, setFlag, setFont, setForeground, setMaximumSize, setMinimumSize, setNextFocusableComponent, setOpaque, setPaintingChild, setPreferredSize, setRequestFocusEnabled, setToolTipText, setUI, setVisible, shouldDebugGraphics, superProcessMouseMotionEvent, unregisterKeyboardAction, unregisterWithKeyboardManager, update

Methods inherited from class java.awt.Container

add, add, add, add, add, addContainerListener, addImpl, applyOrientation, countComponents, deliverEvent, dispatchEventImpl, dispatchEventToSelf, doLayout, eventEnabled, findComponentAt, findComponentAt, getComponent, getComponentAt, getComponentAt, getComponentCount, getComponents_NoClientCode, getComponents, getCursorTarget, getLayout, getMouseEventTarget, getWindow, initIDs, insets, invalidate, invalidateTree, isAncestorOf, layout, lightweightPrint, list, list, locate, minimumSize, nextFocus, paintComponents, postProcessKeyEvent, postsOldMouseEvents, preferredSize, preProcessKeyEvent, printComponents, printHeavyweightComponents, printOneComponent, processContainerEvent, processEvent, proxyEnableEvents, proxyRequestFocus, remove, remove, removeAll, removeContainerListener, setCursor, setFocusOwner, setLayout, transferFocus, updateCursor, validate, validateTree

Methods inherited from class java.awt.Component

action, add, addComponentListener, addFocusListener, addInputMethodListener, addKeyListener, addMouseListener, addMouseMotionListener, areInputMethodsEnabled, bounds, checkImage, checkImage, coalesceEvents, constructComponentName, contains, createImage, createImage, disable, disableEvents, dispatchEvent, enable, enable, enableEvents, enableInputMethods, getBackground, getBounds, getColorModel, getComponentOrientation, getCursor, getDropTarget, getFont_NoClientCode, getFont, getFontMetrics, getForeground, getInputContext, getInputMethodRequests, getIntrinsicCursor, getLocale, getLocation, getLocationOnScreen, getName, getNativeContainer, getParent_NoClientCode, getParent, getPeer, getSize, getToolkit, getToolkitImpl, getTreeLock, getWindowForObject, gotFocus, handleEvent, hide, imageUpdate, inside, isDisplayable, isEnabled, isEnabledImpl, isLightweight, isShowing, isValid, isVisible, keyDown, keyUp, list, list, list, location, lostFocus, mouseDown, mouseDrag, mouseEnter, mouseExit, mouseMove, mouseUp, move, nextFocus, paintAll, postEvent, prepareImage, prepareImage, processComponentEvent, processInputMethodEvent, processMouseEvent, remove, removeComponentListener, removeFocusListener, removeInputMethodListener, removeKeyListener, removeMouseListener, removeMouseMotionListener, repaint, repaint, repaint, resize, resize, setBounds, setBounds, setComponentOrientation, setDropTarget, setLocale, setLocation, setLocation, setName, setSize, setSize, show, show, size, toString, transferFocus

Methods inherited from class java.lang.Object

clone, equals, finalize, getClass, hashCode, notify, notifyAll, registerNatives, wait, wait, wait

Field Detail

unitdb

UnitDb **unitdb**

TOP_NODE

UnitNode **TOP_NODE**

SWING RMI CLIENT

LAST_NODE

UnitNode **LAST_NODE**

TOP_TREE

public javax.swing.tree.DefaultMutableTreeNode **TOP_TREE**

tree

public javax.swing.JTree **tree**

TSL

javax.swing.event.TreeSelectionListener **TSL**

treeview

javax.swing.JScrollPane **treeview**

Constructor Detail

UnitTreeBrowser

public **UnitTreeBrowser**(UnitDb u)

Method Detail

addTreeListener

public void **addTreeListener**(javax.swing.event.TreeSelectionListener t)

createNodes

public void **createNodes**(javax.swing.tree.DefaultMutableTreeNode top)

main

public static void **main**(java.lang.String[] args)

Class GetImageServlet

```
java.lang.Object
  |
  +--javax.servlet.GenericServlet
       |
       +--javax.servlet.http.HttpServlet
            |
            +--GetImageServlet
```

public class **GetImageServlet**
extends javax.servlet.http.HttpServlet

See Also:
> *Serialized Form*

Field Summary

(package private) java.sql.Connection	**conn**
(package private) java.lang.String	**url**

Fields inherited from class javax.servlet.GenericServlet

config

Constructor Summary

GetImageServlet()

Method Summary

void	**doGet**(javax.servlet.http.HttpServletRequest req, javax.servlet.http.HttpServletResponse res) This servlet expects the 'unitid' key-value pair to be part of the QUERY_STRING.
void	**getImageForWeb**(int imageid, javax.servlet.ServletOutputStream out) The imageid and ServletOutputStream are passed in so that the BLOB can be read from the database and then written to the output stream of the servlet as bytes.
java.lang.String[]	**getImageId**(int unitid) This returns a string array containing all the keys to the images that may belong to a single entry in the database.
java.lang.String	**getServletInfo**()
void	**init**(javax.servlet.ServletConfig config) The init method opens up a database connection and logs it.

Methods inherited from class javax.servlet.http.HttpServlet

doDelete, doHead, doOptions, doPost, doPut, doTrace, getAllDeclaredMethods, getLastModified, maybeSetLastModified, service, service

Methods inherited from class javax.servlet.GenericServlet

destroy, getInitParameter, getInitParameterNames, getServletConfig, getServletContext, log

Methods inherited from class java.lang.Object

clone, equals, finalize, getClass, hashCode, notify, notifyAll, registerNatives, toString, wait, wait, wait

Field Detail

conn

java.sql.Connection **conn**

url

java.lang.String **url**

Constructor Detail

GetImageServlet

public **GetImageServlet**()

Method Detail

init

```
public void init(javax.servlet.ServletConfig config)
        throws javax.servlet.ServletException
```

> The init method opens up a database connection and logs it.
> **Overrides:**
> > init in class javax.servlet.GenericServlet
> **Parameters:**
> > config - a value of type 'ServletConfig'
> **Throws:**
> > javax.servlet.ServletException - if an error occurs
> > if - an error occurs

doGet

```
public void doGet(javax.servlet.http.HttpServletRequest req,
                  javax.servlet.http.HttpServletResponse res)
        throws javax.servlet.ServletException,
               java.io.IOException
```

> This servlet expects the 'unitid' key-value pair to be part of the QUERY_STRING. It uses the value to make a database query and find the correct record by calling getImageForWeb().
> **Overrides:**
> > doGet in class javax.servlet.http.HttpServlet
> **Parameters:**
> > req - a value of type 'HttpServletRequest'
> > res - a value of type 'HttpServletResponse'
> **Throws:**
> > javax.servlet.ServletException - if an error occurs
> > java.io.IOException - if an error occurs
> > if - an error occurs

getImageForWeb

```
public void getImageForWeb(int imageid,
                           javax.servlet.ServletOutputStream out)
```

> The imageid and ServletOutputStream are passed in so that the BLOB can be read from the database and then written to the output stream of the servlet as bytes.
> **Parameters:**
> > imageid - a value of type 'int'
> > out - a value of type 'ServletOutputStream'

WEB CLIENT

getImageId

`public java.lang.String[] getImageId (int unitid)`

This returns a string array containing all the keys to the images that may belong to a single entry in the database.

Parameters:
> unitid - a value of type 'int'

Returns:
> a value of type 'String'

getServletInfo

`public java.lang.String getServletInfo()`

Overrides:
> getServletInfo in class javax.servlet.GenericServlet

Class ImageServlet

```
java.lang.Object
  |
  +--javax.servlet.GenericServlet
        |
        +--javax.servlet.http.HttpServlet
              |
              +--ImageServlet
```

public class **ImageServlet**
extends javax.servlet.http.HttpServlet

ImageServlet.java Created: Fri Dec 3 22:35:17 1999

Version:
> 1.0 This servlet handles inserting images into the database as BLOBs. (Binary Large OBjects). The doGet method returns the form used to upload the image. The doPost method reads the MultiPart Form Encoding and inserts the image into the database. It also returns the image uploaded for confirmation. This servlet also calls the UnitDbImpl object directly, thus holding its own database connection rather than using the remote object. This serves as an example of using the API directly for performance/load balancing reasons.

Author:
> (c) 1999, 2000 Stewart Birnam

See Also:
> *Serialized Form*

Field Summary

(package private) UnitDbImpl	`unitdb`

Fields inherited from class javax.servlet.GenericServlet

`config`

Constructor Summary

`ImageServlet()`

Method Summary

void	**doGet**(javax.servlet.http.HttpServletRequest req, javax.servlet.http.HttpServletResponse res) This method generates the form required for the doPost method.
void	**doPost**(javax.servlet.http.HttpServletRequest req, javax.servlet.http.HttpServletResponse res) doPost decodes the MultiPart form data and inserts a new Image into the database.
java.lang.String	**getBoundry**(java.lang.String s) a utility method for determining the actual form boundry.
java.lang.String	**getServletInfo**()
void	**init**(javax.servlet.ServletConfig config)

Methods inherited from class javax.servlet.http.HttpServlet

doDelete, doHead, doOptions, doPut, doTrace, getAllDeclaredMethods, getLastModified, maybeSetLastModified, service, service

Methods inherited from class javax.servlet.GenericServlet

destroy, getInitParameter, getInitParameterNames, getServletConfig, getServletContext, log

Methods inherited from class java.lang.Object

clone, equals, finalize, getClass, hashCode, notify, notifyAll, registerNatives, toString, wait, wait, wait

Field Detail

unitdb

UnitDbImpl **unitdb**

Constructor Detail

ImageServlet

public **ImageServlet**()

Method Detail

init

public void **init**(javax.servlet.ServletConfig config)
     throws javax.servlet.ServletException

Overrides:
    init in class javax.servlet.GenericServlet

---

doGet

```
public void doGet(javax.servlet.http.HttpServletRequest req,
                  javax.servlet.http.HttpServletResponse res)
           throws javax.servlet.ServletException,
                  java.io.IOException
```

This method generates the form required for the doPost method. It requires that the unitid be passed in. The calling URL would be /servlets/ImageServlet?unitid=XXX.
Overrides:
    doGet in class javax.servlet.http.HttpServlet
Parameters:
    req - a value of type 'HttpServletRequest'
    res - a value of type 'HttpServletResponse'
Throws:
    javax.servlet.ServletException - if an error occurs
    java.io.IOException - if an error occurs
    if - an error occurs

---

doPost

```
public void doPost(javax.servlet.http.HttpServletRequest req,
                   javax.servlet.http.HttpServletResponse res)
            throws javax.servlet.ServletException,
                   java.io.IOException
```

doPost decodes the MultiPart form data and inserts a new Image into the database. It returns the uploaded image as selected out of the database to the browser as confirmation.
Overrides:
    doPost in class javax.servlet.http.HttpServlet
Parameters:
    req - a value of type 'HttpServletRequest'
    res - a value of type 'HttpServletResponse'
Throws:
    javax.servlet.ServletException - if an error occurs
    java.io.IOException - if an error occurs
    if - an error occurs

WEB CLIENT

---

getBoundry

```
public java.lang.String getBoundry(java.lang.String s)
```

a utility method for determining the actual form boundry.
Parameters:
    s - a value of type 'String'
Returns:
    a value of type 'String'

getServletInfo

`public java.lang.String getServletInfo()`

> **Overrides:**
>> getServletInfo in class javax.servlet.GenericServlet

Class MultiPartReader

```
java.lang.Object
  |
  +--MultiPartReader
```

public class **MultiPartReader**
extends java.lang.Object

MultiPartReader.java Created: Tue Nov 30 22:30:13 1999 This object reads the data from a Multi-part encoded form post and returns a Hashtable. This is specially designed to deal with binary data, as in an image file upload.

Version:
  1.0
Author:
  (c) 1999, 2000 Stewart Birnam

Field Summary

(package private) javax.servlet.http.HttpServletRequest	**req**

Constructor Summary

MultiPartReader(javax.servlet.http.HttpServletRequest r)

Method Summary

java.lang.String	**getBoundry**(java.lang.String s)
java.util.Hashtable	**getFormData**() This returns a Hashtable with the keys being the names used in the HTML form for each form element.

Methods inherited from class java.lang.Object
clone, equals, finalize, getClass, hashCode, notify, notifyAll, registerNatives, toString, wait, wait, wait

WEB CLIENT

Field Detail

req

```
javax.servlet.http.HttpServletRequest req
```

Constructor Detail

MultiPartReader

```
public MultiPartReader(javax.servlet.http.HttpServletRequest r)
```

Method Detail

getFormData

```
public java.util.Hashtable getFormData()
                           throws java.io.IOException
```

> This returns a Hashtable with the keys being the names used in the HTML form for each form element.
> **Parameters:**
> > `nil` - a value of type "
> **Returns:**
> > a value of type 'Hashtable'
> **Throws:**
> > java.io.IOException - if an error occurs
> > if - an error occurs

---

getBoundry

```
public java.lang.String getBoundry(java.lang.String s)
```

Class UnitDbServlet

```
java.lang.Object
  |
  +--javax.servlet.GenericServlet
        |
        +--javax.servlet.http.HttpServlet
              |
              +--UnitDbServlet
```

public class **UnitDbServlet**
extends javax.servlet.http.HttpServlet

UnitDbServlet.java Created: Thu Nov 11 17:33:19 1999

Version:
    1.0
Author:
    (c)1999, 2000 Stewart Birnam
See Also:
    Serialized Form

WEB CLIENT

Field Summary

(package private) java.util.Hashtable	**colorhash**
(package private) java.util.Hashtable	**coloridhash**
(package private) java.util.Hashtable	**mfghash**
(package private) java.util.Hashtable	**mfgidhash**
(package private) java.lang.String	**RMIHOST**
(package private) java.lang.String	**RMINAME**
(package private) java.lang.String	**SERVLET**
(package private) UnitDb	**unitdb**
(package private) java.lang.String	**url**

Fields inherited from class javax.servlet.GenericServlet

config

Constructor Summary

UnitDbServlet()

Method Summary

void	**doGet**(javax.servlet.http.HttpServletRequest req, javax.servlet.http.HttpServletResponse res)
java.lang.String	**fontize**(java.lang.String s)
java.lang.String	**getServletInfo**()
void	**httpError**(java.lang.Exception e, javax.servlet.ServletOutputStream out) This method will report any errors directly to the web browser, rather than ending up in a server log somewhere.
void	**init**(javax.servlet.ServletConfig config)
void	**initRMI**()
void	**loadHash**()
java.lang.String	**printHeader**()
void	**printUnits**(javax.servlet.ServletOutputStream out, int parentid)
void	**unitDetail**(javax.servlet.ServletOutputStream out, int id) unitDetail extracts all the pertinent data from the UnitInfo object that it retrieves from the unitdb object, and writes it out as a HTML table.

Methods inherited from class javax.servlet.http.HttpServlet

doDelete, doHead, doOptions, doPost, doPut, doTrace, getAllDeclaredMethods, getLastModified, maybeSetLastModified, service, service

Methods inherited from class javax.servlet.GenericServlet

destroy, getInitParameter, getInitParameterNames, getServletConfig, getServletContext, log

Methods inherited from class java.lang.Object

clone, equals, finalize, getClass, hashCode, notify, notifyAll, registerNatives, toString, wait, wait, wait

Field Detail

url

java.lang.String **url**

WEB CLIENT

RMINAME

`java.lang.String` **`RMINAME`**

RMIHOST

`java.lang.String` **`RMIHOST`**

---

unitdb

`UnitDb` **`unitdb`**

SERVLET

`java.lang.String` **`SERVLET`**

---

colorhash

`java.util.Hashtable` **`colorhash`**

---

mfghash

`java.util.Hashtable` **`mfghash`**

---

coloridhash

`java.util.Hashtable` **`coloridhash`**

---

mfgidhash

`java.util.Hashtable` **`mfgidhash`**

Constructor Detail

UnitDbServlet

`public` **`UnitDbServlet`**`()`

Method Detail

init

```
public void init(javax.servlet.ServletConfig config)
        throws javax.servlet.ServletException
```

> **Overrides:**
> init in class javax.servlet.GenericServlet

initRMI

```
public void initRMI()
```

loadHash

```
public void loadHash()
```

doGet

```
public void doGet(javax.servlet.http.HttpServletRequest req,
                  javax.servlet.http.HttpServletResponse res)
        throws javax.servlet.ServletException,
               java.io.IOException
```

> **Overrides:**
> doGet in class javax.servlet.http.HttpServlet

printUnits

```
public void printUnits(javax.servlet.ServletOutputStream out,
                       int parentid)
```

unitDetail

```
public void unitDetail(javax.servlet.ServletOutputStream out,
                       int id)
```

> unitDetail extracts all the pertinent data from the UnitInfo object that it retrieves from the unitdb object, and writes it out as a HTML table.
> **Parameters:**
> out - a value of type 'ServletOutputStream'
> id - a value of type 'int'

WEB CLIENT

getServletInfo

```
public java.lang.String getServletInfo()
```
> **Overrides:**
>> getServletInfo in class javax.servlet.GenericServlet

printHeader

```
public java.lang.String printHeader()
```

fontize

```
public java.lang.String fontize(java.lang.String s)
```

httpError

```
public void httpError(java.lang.Exception e,
                      javax.servlet.ServletOutputStream out)
```

This method will report any errors directly to the web browser, rather than ending up in a server log somewhere. Very useful for debugging and handling errors that we can predict. Notice that you can also allow the user to make method calls by providing links that pass back in values you can act on. The link printed in the method would force the servlet to reinitialize its RMI object by calling initRMI() from doGet().

Parameters:
> e - a value of type 'Exception'
> out - a value of type 'ServletOutputStream'

Class UnitDbCmdLin

```
java.lang.Object
   |
   +--UnitDbCmdLin
```

public class **UnitDbCmdLin**
extends java.lang.Object

UnitDbCmdLin.java Created: Wed Dec 29 22:58:15 1999

The command line client that uses RMI to talk to the database via the UnitDb interface.

Version:
      1.0
Author:
      (c) 1999, 2000 Stewart Birnam

Field Summary

(package private) java.lang.String	**delimiter**
(package private) UnitDb	**unitdb**

Constructor Summary

UnitDbCmdLin()
UnitDbCmdLin(java.lang.String rmihost, java.lang.String rminame)

Method Summary

void	**findByColor**(java.lang.String c)
void	**initRMI**(java.lang.String rmihost, java.lang.String rminame)
static void	**main**(java.lang.String[] args)
void	**setDelimiter**(java.lang.String d)

Methods inherited from class java.lang.Object

clone, equals, finalize, getClass, hashCode, notify, notifyAll, registerNatives, toString, wait, wait, wait

Field Detail

unitdb

UnitDb **unitdb**

---

delimiter

java.lang.String **delimiter**

Constructor Detail

UnitDbCmdLin

public **UnitDbCmdLin**()

UnitDbCmdLin

public **UnitDbCmdLin**(java.lang.String rmihost,
                   java.lang.String rminame)

Method Detail

initRMI

public void **initRMI**(java.lang.String rmihost,
                   java.lang.String rminame)

setDelimiter

```
public void setDelimiter(java.lang.String d)
```

findByColor

```
public void findByColor(java.lang.String c)
```

main

```
public static void main(java.lang.String[] args)
```

Class MonitorPanel

```
java.lang.Object
   |
   +--java.awt.Component
        |
        +--java.awt.Container
              |
              +--javax.swing.JComponent
                    |
                    +--javax.swing.JPanel
                          |
                          +--MonitorPanel
```

public class **MonitorPanel**
extends javax.swing.JPanel
implements java.lang.Runnable

MonitorPanel.java Created: Sun Jan 23 22:26:50 2000

Version:
    1.0

    This is a GUI containter for the RMI object ShellCommand that executes a remote 'uptime' for us. This GUI
    uses the information returned from the RMI object to draw an animated load graph.
Author:
    (c) 1999, 2000 Stewart Birnam
See Also:
    Serialized Form

Inner classes inherited from class javax.swing.JPanel
`javax.swing.JPanel.AccessibleJPanel`

Inner classes inherited from class javax.swing.JComponent
`javax.swing.JComponent.AccessibleJComponent`, `javax.swing.JComponent.IntVector`, `javax.swing.JComponent.KeyboardBinding`, `javax.swing.JComponent.KeyboardState`

Inner classes inherited from class java.awt.Component
`java.awt.Component.AWTTreeLock`

Field Summary

(package private) java.awt.Graphics	**buff_graphics**
(package private) java.awt.Image	**buff_image**
(package private) java.awt.FontMetrics	**fm**
(package private) int	**height**
(package private) java.util.Vector	**load1**
(package private) java.util.Vector	**load2**
(package private) java.util.Vector	**load3**
(package private) ShellCommand	**shellcommand**
(package private) java.lang.Thread	**thread**
(package private) int	**width**

Fields inherited from class javax.swing.JPanel

defaultLayout, uiClassID

Fields inherited from class javax.swing.JComponent

_bounds, accessibleContext, alignmentX, alignmentY, ANCESTOR_USING_BUFFER,
ancestorNotifier, autoscroller, border, changeSupport, clientProperties, flags, HAS_FOCUS,
IS_DOUBLE_BUFFERED, IS_OPAQUE, IS_PAINTING_TILE, IS_PRINTING, IS_PRINTING_ALL,
KEYBOARD_BINDINGS_KEY, listenerList, maximumSize, minimumSize, NEXT_FOCUS,
paintImmediatelyClip, paintingChild, preferredSize, readObjectCallbacks,
REQUEST_FOCUS_DISABLED, tmpRect, TOOL_TIP_TEXT_KEY, ui, uiClassID, UNDEFINED_CONDITION,
vetoableChangeSupport, WHEN_ANCESTOR_OF_FOCUSED_COMPONENT, WHEN_FOCUSED,
WHEN_IN_FOCUSED_WINDOW

Fields inherited from class java.awt.Container

component, containerListener, containerSerializedDataVersion, dispatcher, layoutMgr,
maxSize, ncomponents, serialVersionUID

Fields inherited from class java.awt.Component
actionListenerK, adjustmentListenerK, appContext, assert, background, BOTTOM_ALIGNMENT, CENTER_ALIGNMENT, changeSupport, componentListener, componentListenerK, componentOrientation, componentSerializedDataVersion, containerListenerK, cursor, dropTarget, enabled, eventMask, focusListener, focusListenerK, font, foreground, hasFocus, height, incRate, inputMethodListener, inputMethodListenerK, isInc, isPacked, itemListenerK, keyListener, keyListenerK, LEFT_ALIGNMENT, locale, LOCK, minSize, mouseListener, mouseListenerK, mouseMotionListener, mouseMotionListenerK, name, nameExplicitlySet, newEventsOnly, ownedWindowK, parent, peer, peerFont, popups, prefSize, RIGHT_ALIGNMENT, serialVersionUID, textListenerK, TOP_ALIGNMENT, valid, visible, width, windowListenerK, x, y

Constructor Summary

MonitorPanel()

Method Summary

static void	**main**(java.lang.String[] args)
void	**paint**(java.awt.Graphics g) Draws our backing store to the screen.
void	**run**() All the animation work is done here, as well as the call to the remote object to get the latest values.
void	**start**() Starts the animation thread.
void	**stop**() Stops the animation thread.

Methods inherited from class javax.swing.JPanel
getAccessibleContext, getUIClassID, paramString, updateUI, writeObject

Methods inherited from class javax.swing.JComponent

_paintImmediately, addAncestorListener, addNotify, addPropertyChangeListener,
addPropertyChangeListener, addVetoableChangeListener, adjustPaintFlags, alwaysOnTop,
bindingForKeyStroke, checkIfChildObscuredBySibling, computeVisibleRect, computeVisibleRect,
contains, createToolTip, enableSerialization, firePropertyChange, firePropertyChange,
firePropertyChange, firePropertyChange, firePropertyChange, firePropertyChange,
firePropertyChange, firePropertyChange, firePropertyChange, fireVetoableChange,
getActionForKeyStroke, getAlignmentX, getAlignmentY, getAutoscrolls, getBorder, getBounds,
getClientProperties, getClientProperty, getComponentGraphics, getConditionForKeyStroke,
getDebugGraphicsOptions, getFlag, getGraphics, getHeight, getInsets, getInsets,
getLocation, getMaximumSize, getMinimumSize, getNextFocusableComponent, getPreferredSize,
getRegisteredKeyStrokes, getRootPane, getSize, getToolTipLocation, getToolTipText,
getToolTipText, getTopLevelAncestor, getVisibleRect, getWidth, getX, getY, grabFocus,
hasFocus, isDoubleBuffered, isFocusCycleRoot, isFocusTraversable, isLightweightComponent,
isManagingFocus, isOpaque, isOptimizedDrawingEnabled, isPaintingTile,
isRequestFocusEnabled, isValidateRoot, keyboardBindings, paintBorder, paintChildren,
paintComponent, paintImmediately, paintImmediately, paintWithBuffer, print, printAll,
processComponentKeyEvent, processFocusEvent, processKeyBinding, processKeyBindings,
processKeyBindingsForAllComponents, processKeyEvent, processMouseMotionEvent,
putClientProperty, readObject, rectangleIsObscured, rectangleIsObscuredBySibling,
registerKeyboardAction, registerKeyboardAction, registerWithKeyboardManager,
removeAncestorListener, removeNotify, removePropertyChangeListener,
removePropertyChangeListener, removeVetoableChangeListener, repaint, repaint,
requestDefaultFocus, requestFocus, resetKeyboardActions, reshape, revalidate,
scrollRectToVisible, setAlignmentX, setAlignmentY, setAutoscrolls, setBackground,
setBorder, setDebugGraphicsOptions, setDoubleBuffered, setEnabled, setFlag, setFont,
setForeground, setMaximumSize, setMinimumSize, setNextFocusableComponent, setOpaque,
setPaintingChild, setPreferredSize, setRequestFocusEnabled, setToolTipText, setUI,
setVisible, shouldDebugGraphics, superProcessMouseMotionEvent, unregisterKeyboardAction,
unregisterWithKeyboardManager, update

Methods inherited from class java.awt.Container

add, add, add, add, add, addContainerListener, addImpl, applyOrientation, countComponents,
deliverEvent, dispatchEventImpl, dispatchEventToSelf, doLayout, eventEnabled,
findComponentAt, findComponentAt, getComponent, getComponentAt, getComponentAt,
getComponentCount, getComponents_NoClientCode, getComponents, getCursorTarget, getLayout,
getMouseEventTarget, getWindow, initIDs, insets, invalidate, invalidateTree, isAncestorOf,
layout, lightweightPrint, list, list, locate, minimumSize, nextFocus, paintComponents,
postProcessKeyEvent, postsOldMouseEvents, preferredSize, preProcessKeyEvent,
printComponents, printHeavyweightComponents, printOneComponent, processContainerEvent,
processEvent, proxyEnableEvents, proxyRequestFocus, remove, remove, removeAll,
removeContainerListener, setCursor, setFocusOwner, setLayout, transferFocus, updateCursor,
validate, validateTree

Methods inherited from class java.awt.Component

action, add, addComponentListener, addFocusListener, addInputMethodListener, addKeyListener, addMouseListener, addMouseMotionListener, areInputMethodsEnabled, bounds, checkImage, checkImage, coalesceEvents, constructComponentName, contains, createImage, createImage, disable, disableEvents, dispatchEvent, enable, enable, enableEvents, enableInputMethods, getBackground, getBounds, getColorModel, getComponentOrientation, getCursor, getDropTarget, getFont_NoClientCode, getFont, getFontMetrics, getForeground, getInputContext, getInputMethodRequests, getIntrinsicCursor, getLocale, getLocation, getLocationOnScreen, getName, getNativeContainer, getParent_NoClientCode, getParent, getPeer, getSize, getToolkit, getToolkitImpl, getTreeLock, getWindowForObject, gotFocus, handleEvent, hide, imageUpdate, inside, isDisplayable, isEnabled, isEnabledImpl, isLightweight, isShowing, isValid, isVisible, keyDown, keyUp, list, list, list, location, lostFocus, mouseDown, mouseDrag, mouseEnter, mouseExit, mouseMove, mouseUp, move, nextFocus, paintAll, postEvent, prepareImage, prepareImage, processComponentEvent, processInputMethodEvent, processMouseEvent, remove, removeComponentListener, removeFocusListener, removeInputMethodListener, removeKeyListener, removeMouseListener, removeMouseMotionListener, repaint, repaint, repaint, resize, resize, setBounds, setBounds, setComponentOrientation, setDropTarget, setLocale, setLocation, setLocation, setName, setSize, setSize, show, show, size, toString, transferFocus

---

Methods inherited from class java.lang.Object

clone, equals, finalize, getClass, hashCode, notify, notifyAll, registerNatives, wait, wait, wait

---

Field Detail

thread

java.lang.Thread **thread**

---

buff_image

java.awt.Image **buff_image**

---

buff_graphics

java.awt.Graphics **buff_graphics**

---

shellcommand

ShellCommand **shellcommand**

REMOTE MONITORING

width

```
int width
```

height

```
int height
```

load1

```
java.util.Vector load1
```

load2

```
java.util.Vector load2
```

load3

```
java.util.Vector load3
```

fm

```
java.awt.FontMetrics fm
```

Constructor Detail

MonitorPanel

```
public MonitorPanel()
```

Method Detail

start

```
public void start()
```

> Starts the animation thread.
> **Parameters:**
> > nil - a value of type "

stop
```
public void stop()
```

Stops the animation thread.
Parameters:
  `nil` - a value of type "

---

run
```
public void run()
```

All the animation work is done here, as well as the call to the remote object to get the latest values.
Specified by:
  run in interface java.lang.Runnable
Parameters:
  `nil` - a value of type "

---

paint
```
public void paint(java.awt.Graphics g)
```

Draws our backing store to the screen.
Overrides:
  paint in class javax.swing.JComponent
Parameters:
  `g` - a value of type 'Graphics'

---

main
```
public static void main(java.lang.String[] args)
```

Class MonitorServer

```
java.lang.Object
  |
  +--MonitorServer
```

public class **MonitorServer**
extends java.lang.Object

MonitorServer.java Created: Tue Jan 25 22:16:12 2000

A simple class to make the ShellCommandImpl class available via RMI.

The class will name itself in the RMI registery based on the contents of the property monitor.rminame present at runtime.

example: java -Dmonitor.rminame=MONITOR MonitorServer
...will name the class MONITOR in the RMI registry.

Version:
>1.0

Author:
>(c) 1999, 2000 Stewart Birnam

Constructor Summary

MonitorServer()

Method Summary

static void	**main**(java.lang.String[] args)

Methods inherited from class java.lang.Object

clone, equals, finalize, getClass, hashCode, notify, notifyAll, registerNatives, toString, wait, wait, wait

Constructor Detail

MonitorServer

```
public MonitorServer()
```

Method Detail

main

```
public static void main(java.lang.String[] args)
```

Interface ShellCommand

All Known Implementing Classes:
  ShellCommandImpl

---

public interface **ShellCommand**
extends java.rmi.Remote

ShellCommand.java Created: Sun Jan 23 18:22:03 2000

The interface for the Remote Object.

Version:
  1.0
Author:
  Stewart Birnam

Method Summary

`java.lang.String[]`	`getLoad()`

Method Detail

getLoad

```
public java.lang.String[] getLoad()
                    throws java.rmi.RemoteException
```

Class ShellCommandImpl

```
java.lang.Object
  |
  +--java.rmi.server.RemoteObject
       |
       +--java.rmi.server.RemoteServer
            |
            +--java.rmi.server.UnicastRemoteObject
                 |
                 +--ShellCommandImpl
```

public class **ShellCommandImpl**
extends java.rmi.server.UnicastRemoteObject
implements *ShellCommand*

ShellCommandImpl.java Created: Sun Jan 23 18:24:42 2000

Version:
    1.0
Author:
    (c)1999, 2000 Stewart Birnam
See Also:
    Serialized Form

Fields inherited from class java.rmi.server.UnicastRemoteObject

csf, port, portFactoryParamTypes, portParamTypes, serialVersionUID, ssf

---

Fields inherited from class java.rmi.server.RemoteServer

log, logname, serialVersionUID

Fields inherited from class java.rmi.server.RemoteObject

ref, serialVersionUID

Constructor Summary

ShellCommandImpl()
    The Implementation class for executing commands on remote system via RMI.

Method Summary

private java.lang.String	**execCommand**(java.lang.String s) This method exeecutes the command passed into it.
java.lang.String[]	**getLoad**() This method calls execCommand() with a set String compiled in and thus 'safe' at least as far as we're concerned.
static void	**main**(java.lang.String[] args) A test method to validate results.

Methods inherited from class java.rmi.server.UnicastRemoteObject

clone, exportObject, exportObject, exportObject, exportObject, readObject, reexport, unexportObject

Methods inherited from class java.rmi.server.RemoteServer

getClientHost, getLog, setLog

Methods inherited from class java.rmi.server.RemoteObject

equals, getRef, hashCode, toString, toStub, writeObject

Methods inherited from class java.lang.Object

finalize, getClass, notify, notifyAll, registerNatives, wait, wait, wait

Constructor Detail

ShellCommandImpl

```
public ShellCommandImpl()
                throws java.rmi.RemoteException
```

The Implementation class for executing commands on remote system via RMI.

The constructor could be rewritten to source a properties file that would restrict the types of commands that it could run, or limit the path to certain binaries.
Throws:
    java.rmi.RemoteException - if an error occurs

Method Detail

execCommand

```
private java.lang.String execCommand(java.lang.String s)
                      throws java.rmi.RemoteException
```

This method exeecutes the command passed into it. Note that it is private and that public access to this method is controlled by other methods that examine and 'make safe' what is passed in here.

Parameters:
  `s` - a value of type 'String' - the command to run.
Returns:
  a value of type 'String' - the STDOUT or STDERR from the command.
Throws:
  java.rmi.RemoteException - if an error occurs

getLoad

```
public java.lang.String[] getLoad()
                       throws java.rmi.RemoteException
```

This method calls execCommand() with a set String compiled in and thus 'safe' at least as far as we're concerned.

This method assumes the location of uptime as /usr/bin/uptime and how it responds on Redhat Linux 6.1. It then parses the return value from @see execCommand and returns an array of Strings as dictated by the underlying Interface.

You may need to alter this code to run properly on another OS.

Specified by:
  getLoad in interface *ShellCommand*
Parameters:
  `nil` - a value of type "
Returns:
  a value of type 'String'
Throws:
  java.rmi.RemoteException - if an error occurs
  if - an error occurs

main

```
public static void main(java.lang.String[] args)
```

A test method to validate results.

Parameters:
  `args` - a value of type 'String[]'

Class BadWeightException

```
java.lang.Object
  |
  +--java.lang.Throwable
        |
        +--java.lang.Exception
              |
              +--BadWeightException
```

public class **BadWeightException**
extends java.lang.Exception

BadWeightException.java Created: Wed Oct 27 00:05:08 1999

Version:
    1.0
Author:
    (c)1999, 2000 Stewart Birnam
See Also:
    Serialized Form

Fields inherited from class java.lang.Throwable
`backtrace, detailMessage, serialVersionUID`

Constructor Summary

`BadWeightException()`   BadWeightException is just an extension of the base Exception class.

Methods inherited from class java.lang.Throwable
`fillInStackTrace, getLocalizedMessage, getMessage, printStackTrace, printStackTrace, printStackTrace, printStackTrace0, toString`

Methods inherited from class java.lang.Object
`clone, equals, finalize, getClass, hashCode, notify, notifyAll, registerNatives, wait, wait, wait`

UTILITIES

Constructor Detail

BadWeightException

```
public BadWeightException()
```

BadWeightException is just an extension of the base Exception class. This is simply to serve as an example of using the name of the exception to 'tell it all'.

In other cases you may want to pass in a String to the constructor so that someone could call getMessage() on it. However for us, the name says it all.

Class DbUtil

```
java.lang.Object
  |
  +--DbUtil
```

class **DbUtil**
extends java.lang.Object

Field Summary

java.text.SimpleDateFormat	**formatter**

Constructor Summary

(package private)	**DbUtil**()

Method Summary

java.lang.String	**oraDate**(java.util.Date d) oraDate like oraParse saves us some typing by converting a java.Date object into the format Oracle wants when inserting records.
static java.lang.String	**oraParse**(java.lang.String s) oraParse returns a String bound with single quotes and with any single quote that may appear in the String doubled.
static java.lang.String	**parse**(java.lang.String s, java.lang.String d)

Methods inherited from class java.lang.Object

clone, equals, finalize, getClass, hashCode, notify, notifyAll, registerNatives, toString, wait, wait, wait

Field Detail

formatter

public java.text.SimpleDateFormat **formatter**

UTILITIES

Constructor Detail

DbUtil

```
DbUtil()
```

Method Detail

parse

```
public static java.lang.String parse(java.lang.String s,
                                     java.lang.String d)
```

---

oraParse

```
public static java.lang.String oraParse(java.lang.String s)
```

> oraParse returns a String bound with single quotes and with any single quote that may appear in the String doubled. This makes it ready for insertion into an Oracle database.
> **Parameters:**
>   s - a value of type 'String' example: Alice's Restaurant
> **Returns:**
>   a value of type 'String' example: 'Alice''s Restaurant

---

oraDate

```
public java.lang.String oraDate(java.util.Date d)
```

> oraDate like oraParse saves us some typing by converting a java.Date object into the format Oracle wants when inserting records.
>
> **Parameters:**
>   d - a value of type 'Date'
> **Returns:**
>   a value of type 'String'

Class QSort

```
java.lang.Object
   |
   +--QSort
```

public class **QSort**
extends java.lang.Object

A Object sensitive quick sort algorithm for Vectors.

This was built by hacking the QuickSort demo provided with the JDK to get the basic sorting algorithm.

What we changed was unhooking it from the applet GUI framework it was designed for and making it sensitive to different datatypes, i.e., Date, Number, String, Object, so that those would sort properly.

This class sorts an index and returns it rather than actually reorder a vector, similar in the way a database indexes records.

Version:
    1.0
Author:
    Stewart Birnam

Field Summary

(package private) int []	**index**
(package private) java.lang.Class	**type**
(package private) java.util.Vector	**vec**

Constructor Summary

QSort(java.util.Vector v)
QSort(java.util.Vector v, java.lang.Class t)   QSort takes a vector and classtype describing what the vector contains.

UTILITIES

Method Summary

int	**compareByClass**(java.lang.Object obj1, java.lang.Object obj2, java.lang.Class type)
int[]	**getIndex**()
java.util.Vector	**getSortedVector**()
private void	**initIndex**()
static void	**main**(java.lang.String[] args)
void	**quickSort**(int lo0, int hi0) The quick sort implementation, sensitive to object types.
void	**setType**(java.lang.Class t)
void	**setVector**(java.util.Vector v)
int[]	**sort**()
private void	**swap**(int i, int j)

Methods inherited from class java.lang.Object

clone, equals, finalize, getClass, hashCode, notify, notifyAll, registerNatives, toString, wait, wait, wait

Field Detail

index

int[] **index**

---

vec

java.util.Vector **vec**

---

type

java.lang.Class **type**

Constructor Detail

QSort

```
public QSort(java.util.Vector v)
```

QSort

```
public QSort(java.util.Vector v,
             java.lang.Class t)
```

QSort takes a vector and classtype describing what the vector contains. This insures that the vector is sorted properly. The invocation would look something like this:

```
try {
    QSort q = new Qsort(myvector, Class.forName("java.lang.String"));
}
catch (ClassNotFoundException c) { c.printStactTrace(); }
```

the exception handling is required by the forName method call.

Parameters:
>   v - a value of type 'Vector'
>   type - a value of type 'Class'

Method Detail

initIndex

```
private void initIndex()
```

---

quickSort

```
public void quickSort(int lo0,
                      int hi0)
```

The quick sort implementation, sensitive to object types. Other algorithms may work faster depending on what you are doing. If you have a faster method, you can insert it into this class and call it instead of quickSort.

Parameters:
>   lo0 - left boundary of the index
>   hi0 - right boundary of the index

---

swap

```
private void swap(int i,
                  int j)
```

UTILITIES

compareByClass

```
public int compareByClass(java.lang.Object obj1,
                          java.lang.Object obj2,
                          java.lang.Class type)
```

sort

```
public int[] sort()
```

getIndex

```
public int[] getIndex()
```

setVector

```
public void setVector(java.util.Vector v)
```

setType

```
public void setType(java.lang.Class t)
```

getSortedVector

```
public java.util.Vector getSortedVector()
```

main

```
public static void main(java.lang.String[] args)
```

Class StringSplitter

```
java.lang.Object
   |
   +--StringSplitter
```

public class **StringSplitter**
extends java.lang.Object

StringSplitter.java Created: Sat Nov 27 09:18:09 1999

This class is much like StringTokenizer except it lets you use any length string to delimit with.

Version:
> 1.0

Author:
> (c) 1999, 2000 Stewart Birnam

Field Summary

(package private) java.lang.String	**delimiter**
(package private) int	**start_delim**
(package private) int	**start_position**
(package private) java.lang.String	**str**

Constructor Summary

StringSplitter(java.lang.String s, java.lang.String d)

Method Summary

static void	**main**(java.lang.String[] args)
java.lang.String	**nextToken**()

UTILITIES

Methods inherited from class java.lang.Object
clone, equals, finalize, getClass, hashCode, notify, notifyAll, registerNatives, toString, wait, wait, wait

Field Detail

str

`java.lang.String str`

---

delimiter

`java.lang.String delimiter`

---

start_position

`int start_position`

---

start_delim

`int start_delim`

Constructor Detail

StringSplitter

```
public StringSplitter(java.lang.String s,
                      java.lang.String d)
```

> **Parameters:**
> s - a value of type 'String', what you want to split up
> d - a value of type 'String', the delimiter to split by

Method Detail

nextToken

`public java.lang.String nextToken()`

---

main

`public static void main(java.lang.String[] args)`

Appendix **B**

SQL for Creating the Schema Used in This Book

```
CREATE TABLE UNIT (
    ID       NUMBER constraint pk_unit primary key,
    PARENTID NUMBER,
    NAME     VARCHAR2(30),
    PARTNO   VARCHAR2(10),
    SERIALNO VARCHAR2(10),
    WEIGHT   NUMBER,
    COLOR    NUMBER,
    MFG      NUMBER,
    CDATE    DATE,
    MDATE    DATE,
constraint fk_unit foreign key (PARENTID)
references UNIT (ID)
)
/
CREATE TABLE MFG (
    ID   NUMBER constraint pk_mfg primary key,
    NAME VARCHAR2(30)
)
/
CREATE TABLE QTY (
    ID       NUMBER constraint pk_qty primary key,
    QUANTITY NUMBER
)
/
CREATE TABLE COLOR (
    ID   NUMBER constraint pk_color primary key,
    NAME VARCHAR2(20)
)
/
/*------------------------------------------------------------------*
 * set up foreign key relations back to the UNIT table
 *------------------------------------------------------------------*/
alter table unit add constraint fk_mfg foreign key (MFG)
references MFG (ID);
alter table unit add constraint fk_color foreign key (COLOR)
references COLOR (ID);
```

```
alter table qty add constraint fk_unit_qty foreign key (ID)
references UNIT (ID);
/*------------------------------------------------------------------*
* some starter values for color and mfg lookup tables
*------------------------------------------------------------------*/
insert into color values (1, 'Red');
insert into color values (2, 'Yellow');
insert into color values (3, 'Blue');
insert into mfg values (1, 'Tallos Industries');
insert into mfg values (2, 'Gorn Enterprises');
insert into mfg values (3, 'Atoz Inc.');
insert into unit (id, parentid) values (0,0);
create sequence unitseq;
/*------------------------------------------------------------------*
* IMAGE stuff
*------------------------------------------------------------------*/
create table image (
    id      number constraint pk_image primary key,
    unitid number,
    format number,
    image  long raw
)
/
alter table image add constraint fk_image foreign key (unitid)
references unit (id)
/
create table imageformat (
    id   number constraint pk_imageformat primary key,
    name varchar2(10)
)
/
alter table image add constraint fk_imageformat foreign key (format)
references imageformat (id)
/
insert into imageformat values (1,'JPEG');
commit;
```

Appendix C

Example Makefile

```
# EXAMPLE Makefile for Distributed Java 2 Platform Database Development
#
# (c)2000 Stewart Birnam
#
# This is a very simple makefile for a java software project.
# Javac automatically takes care of most dependencies.
# However, a makefile can be very useful when
# distributing your software or for installing classes and html
# files in the right places when developing servlets.
#
# Makefiles can also be handy for auto-checkin via CVS or creating
# jar files.
#
# this enables a system administrator to type:
#
# make all - to build all your classes.
#
# make inst - to install the software in the right place.
#
# make javadoc - to build and install javadoc api docs.
#
# make jar - to create a jar file quickly.
#
# ... again, something they expect and are used to.
#####################################################################
#
# LOCATION DEPENDENT THINGS TO CHANGE
##################################################
# location for your documentation
DOC_HOME=/usr/local/apache/htdocs/javadoc
# your classpath
CLASSPATH=/usr/oracle/jdbc/lib/classes111.zip:.:/usr/JSDK2.0/lib/jsdk.jar
# servlet directory
SERVLET_HOME=/usr/local/apache/servlets
# nfs mountable software repository
NFS_REPOSITORY=/net/boinx/software/unitdb
##################################################
```

```
# DONT CHANGE BELOW THIS LINE
###################################################
# source files organized by project
DB_SRC=UnitDb.java UnitDbImpl.java BadWeightException.java

SWING_CLIENT_SRC=IUDPanel.java UnitNode.java UnitTreeBrowser.java \
UnitDbClient.java

SERVLET_SRC=MultiPartReader.java GetImageServlet.java ImageServlet.java \
UnitDbServlet.java

RMI_SERVER_SRC=UnitDBServer.java

MONITOR_SRC=ShellCommand.java ShellCommandImpl.java MonitorServer.java \
MonitorPanel.java

UTIL_SRC=StringSplitter.java QSort.java DbUtil.java

SRC=BadWeightException.java GetImageServlet.java IUDPanel.java \
ImageServlet.java MonitorPanel.java MonitorServer.java \
MultiPartReader.java QSort.java ShellCommand.java ShellCommandImpl.java \
StringSplitter.java UnitDBServer.java UnitDb.java UnitDbClient.java \
UnitDbCmdLin.java UnitDbImpl.java UnitDbServlet.java UnitInfo.java \
UnitNode.java UnitTreeBrowser.java

# distribution classes
SERVLET_CLASSES=BadWeightException.class DbUtil.class GetImageServlet.class \
ImageServlet.class MultiPartReader.class QSort.class StringSplitter.class \
UnitDb.class UnitDbImpl.class UnitDbServlet.class UnitInfo.class \
UnitDbImpl_Skel.class UnitDbImpl_Stub.class

# you could probably get away with not specifying dependencies, as javac
# will recompile any source that is newer than the corresponding class
# file automatically.
all: $(SRC)
    javac -g -deprecation -classpath $(CLASSPATH) $(SRC)
    rmic UnitDbImpl
    rmic ShellCommandImpl

db: $(DB_SRC)
    javac -g -classpath $(CLASSPATH) $(DB_SRC)
    rmic UnitDbImpl

javadoc:
    javadoc -private -classpath $(CLASSPATH) -d
    $(DOC_HOME) -version -author -use *.java

servlet: $(SERVLET_SRC)
```

```
        javac -g -classpath $(CLASSPATH) $(SERVLET_SRC)

# installs the class files into the servlet directory.
inst:
        cp $(SERVLET_CLASSES) $(SERVLET_HOME)/

# installs into nfs repository
inst_nfs:
        cp *.class $(NFS_REPOSITORY)/lib/
        cp unitdbd $(NFS_REPOSITORY)/etc/init.d/
        cp rmid $(NFS_REPOSITORY)/etc/init.d/
        cp monitord $(NFS_REPOSITORY)/etc/init.d/
        cp unitreport.sh $(NFS_REPOSITORY)/bin/


# creates a JAR file of all our classes
jar:
        jar cvf unitdb.jar *.class
```

Index